THE
DRAMA OF TH[...]

C000214354

A MYSTICAL INTERPRETATION
OF THE GOSPELS,
describing
THE INNER INITIATIONS OF THE MASTER JESUS.

BY

SHABAZ BRITTEN BEST

second edition

FINE BOOKS ORIENTAL LONDON
EAST-WEST PUBLICATIONS FONDS B.V.   THE HAGUE

For publication-, translation- and subsidiary rights (outside the
United Kingdom and S. Africa) please contact: Mirananda
Publishers B.V., Zijdeweg 5a, 2244 BC Wassenaar, The
Netherlands.

ISBN 0.85692.072.X

© 1980 Joyce Sita Best and Virya Helon Best

Manufactured in the Netherlands.
All rights reserved. No part of this book may be reproduced,
stored in a retrieval system or transmitted in any form, by any
means, electronic, electrical, chemical, mechanical, optical, photo-
copying, recording or otherwise, without the prior, written permission of the publisher.

THE DRAMA OF THE SOUL

This work is dedicated to NURIA (Light Bearer), my cherished companion on the Path.

————◆————

To *P.O.M. Inayat Khan.*

Thou, my Master makest earth a Paradise.
Thy thought giveth me unearthly joy,
Thy Light illuminateth my life's path,
Thy words inspire me with divine Wisdom.
I follow in thy footsteps, which lead me to the Eternal Goal.
Friend of the lovers of Truth,
Thou art the prophet of God.

"VADAN."

The words that enlighten the soul
are more precious than jewels.

"GAYAN."

SHABAZ.

CONTENTS

CHAPTER   PAGE

I   THE DRAMA OF THE SOUL   1

II   WAS JESUS THE ORIGINAL AUTHOR OF THE GOSPEL?   7

III   PROLOGUE TO MATTHEW'S GOSPEL   14

IV   MYSTICAL SIGNIFICANCE OF THE NATIVITY STORY   26

V   THE BIRTH OF JESUS   36

VI   REDEMPTION OF MORAL DEBTS   54

VII   WAS JOHN THE BAPTIST REALLY JESUS?   ...   59

VIII   THE TEMPTATION   97

IX   TRANSFIGURATION   108

X   THE MARRIAGE IN CANA   116

XI   THE CRUCIFIXION   125

XII   RESURRECTION AND ASCENSION   148

---❖---

ILLUSTRATIONS

                                       Facing Page

GENEALOGY OF JESUS   17

THE PASSOVER   126

CHAPTER I

THE DRAMA OF THE SOUL

The ever recurring questions that each succeeding generation has asked are : Why did God create the universe ? What is the purpose of human life ? Is there a peaceful destiny pre-ordained for mankind ? If so, what is the best and happiest means of accomplishing this ideal ? A solution to these queries will reveal the drama of the human soul, which contains all possible experiences of life.

Throughout the ages there have been outstanding individuals, wise men, prophets and messengers of God, who have brought to the world answers to these questions. Their explanations were presented in two aspects : First they gave exoteric and ethical teaching of a practical mode of living, based on good-will and co-operation, while arts and crafts were taught openly to the people in order to stimulate progress in worldly affairs. The second form of their message comprised sacred doctrines concerning God, creation, nature, man and the purpose of life, which were only taught in secret to worthy seekers. This esoteric tuition has been known under various names, such as : the Ancient Mysteries, Secret Doctrine, Ageless Wisdom, Vedanta, Yoga, Kabbala, Gnosis, Mysticism, Sufism and Perennial Philosophy. Although each deals with the essential principles of life, the name was changed with the period, locality, method of approach, and also with the application of the teaching, but all are in perfect accord.

Over an extensive period a vast amount of mystery teaching has been given to the Western hemisphere, and it demonstrates

1

that the history of mankind covers many thousand centuries. Previous chapters of human civilization evidently flourished in areas that have long since been submerged, or transformed by the change in the planet's polar axis which caused earlier temperate zones to be covered with ice.

In ancient times each country was free to propound its own spiritual ideals, without question or conflict. In more modern days this principle was admirably acknowledged by the Roman Empire, in the construction of the Pantheon, wherein the deities of various peoples were given equal rank and homage. Mankind still needs an acknowledged unity of religious ideals.

All great teachers of the world have realized the existence of superphysical planes and beings. The essence of their doctrines shows that individual life is constantly progressing to greater heights and wider realms of consciousness, primarily by the natural law of evolution. They taught that this progress can be stimulated and hastened by appropriate knowledge and individual effort. Therefore special tuition and training were given to qualified and zealous aspirants, who, in due course, were initiated into the mysteries of spiritual truth.

What do we understand by the principles of divine wisdom ? First, the Supreme Godhead is the only Infinite, Eternal and Almighty Being, the Omniscient, Compassionate and All-pervading Source of Life, Light and Love, Ageless, Changeless and Formless, the Great Architect and the true Alpha.

Second, in the beginning of manifestation measurable time commenced as a part of eternity, and the First Emanation of the Godhead, His Beloved Son, was empowered to carry into effect the divine Plan of Creation. He thus became the Creator and Builder of the Cosmos, the Father of all embodied life.

Third, the creative plan of life has a purpose and destiny, based on the principles of Love, Lover and Beloved ; the

Supreme Love of the Godhead embraces mankind as the great lover, together with the Creator as the Beloved Ideal. By virtue of these triple aspects of love, there is a constant approach between the lover and the Beloved, until both become reunited into the ONE. This constitutes the drama of Creation.

Every human being is at some definite stage of progress, having already passed through infinite grades of consciousness, and is still advancing onwards and upwards, in order to regain the perfect love, wisdom and power of Divinity. Different ways of this attainment are adopted by mankind according to the various tendencies of individuals, but all paths lead to the one and only Goal of Reunion which is pre-ordained by God.

Just as white light, passing through different coloured glass, assumes various hues, so spiritual truth becomes transformed by the place, period or person through whom it is presented. Therefore all religions, philosophies and ideologies are means of explaining and attaining the Divine Ideal ; their respective adherents are each and all justified in their acceptance of, or attitude towards, one or another and so should not be criticized or condemned.

How much more in accord with their declared principles it would be if the great religious institutions of the world would form a universal brotherhood, by acknowledging their points of unity in idealism, rather than emphasizing minor differences in their doctrines and ceremonies ! When all people have a spiritual ideal the affairs of state will be rightly directed for the general welfare of all.   There is one divine urge impelling us all to make peaceful progress towards our predestined goal, each one should comfort and assist others with friendly companionship on the great pilgrimage. This is the manner of saints, sages and mystics in all ages.

The first great lesson taught in the ancient mystery schools was that the human body is the necessary dwelling place of the soul while it is acquiring worldly knowledge and developing the innate faculties that will lead it to perfection. The preparation of this development must begin on the lowest plane of manifestation and proceed upwards, in order that man may understand and master all the seven vehicles of his own being. There is a graduated process of advancement, each plane having a corresponding vehicle of consciousness with its own specific attribute.

Thus, the physical body expresses natural instincts ; the emotions generate impulses and sentiments ; the objective mind develops intelligence ; the subjective mind evokes intuition ; the mystic heart manifests inspiration ; the soul is the source of illumination, and the human spirit is the channel whereby man attains identification with the Divine Being. The first triad constitutes the normal three-dimensional person, the illusory self ; the fourth plane establishes the bridge of enlightenment and transition to the higher self, which comprises the three metaphysical bodies with their respective faculties ; it is the true individual. All systems of training for inner development are directed to these three super-normal attributes. Their gradual unfoldment and function is revealed first in the inspired genius, then in the illuminated sage, and finally in the messenger of God, who manifests conscious at-one-ment with the Divinity.

In the early stages of progress, so long as one's interest and consciousness are centred in the lower self and personality, there is unavoidable discontent and conflict, because the mystery and purpose of life have not been discovered. One's physical existence thus seems almost aimless. The gratification of transient pleasures and the acquisition of possessions still leave one unhappy and dissatisfied. Even when one begins to cross over the bridge to the higher self, doubts and mental problems may assail the seeker, who finds he is taking an unusual course in life that others may not understand or approve of, hence the absolute need for inner conviction and calm courage. The transition may be facilitated if counsel and guidance from an elder brother can be obtained. Then, when one has elevated the directive centre of conduct to the heart plane by altruism, it is said he has begun the journey on the Path of Return to the Father. The work of all religions, mystery schools and secret cults should be to explain these advanced stages of progress, and to guide aspirants through the difficulties and dangers of developing and exercising the functions that pertain to the higher self. Its vehicles are composed of superphysical matter of very fine texture, and therefore are almost inscrutable and uncontrollable in the early stages of unfoldment.

Once we acknowledge this truth and perceive the process of spiritual evolution, it becomes obvious that there is no limit to the possible development of faculties and the expansion of human consciousness. The finest example in history is undoubtedly Jesus Christ, who was not an abnormal being, but a human, born and bred as are all " sons of man." He was exceptional because he unfolded and exercised the faculties of consciousness pertaining to his soul and spirit. By saying : " These things and more shall ye do," he emphasized that others are endowed with the potentiality of development and advancement to the states of impersonal power, illuminated wisdom and universal love.

What happens to those human beings who presumably attain perfection, such as Buddha, Zoroaster, Abraham, Solomon, Jesus and Mohammed ? According to occult doctrines they become Masters and, having acquired full development and control of all their human attributes, they can be delegated to act as Ministers of the Spiritual Hierarchy which governs this planet.

Like every large business institution or nation, there must be a board of directors, or cabinet with executive heads, who are responsible for the wise and successful direction of the world. Consequently there is an invisible spiritual government, directed by qualified administrators, who are potent

influences in the affairs of all nations.   They silently guide and
encourage man's co-operation in all branches of human
activity, such as agriculture, industry, science, art, philosophy,
religion and the deeper mystery teachings.   One Master may
be given charge over each department, but they all work in
co-ordination with more advanced beings, such as the Manu,
or Race Builder, and the Christ, or World Teacher.   Above
them all is the Planetary Lord, who is the Guiding Spirit of
all mankind, beyond race, creed or colour.   All together
constitute the Spiritual Hierarchy of this earth.   Naturally
there are similar Hierarchies in charge of other planets.   The
head of each becomes *ex officio* a member of the Solar Hierarchy,
so that the entire solar system is governed as one co-operative
unit under the leadership of the Solar Logos, who is the primary aspect of our Heavenly Father.

Beyond this mighty Celestial Being there are still higher
Constellatory Logoi, all of whom work in harmony with the
Great Father-Mother, the Creative Deity and Builder of all
universes.   He is the " Alone Begotten," the First Manifestation of the Absolute Godhead Who is the Controller of
the entire Cosmos, but of Whom naught can be said, because
He is Unconditioned and without attributes, the LIGHT of
all lesser Lights and the One Source of all Life, " in Whom we
live and move and have our being."

So we humans can never cease to exist within the limits of
infinite space and eternity of time ; but we have comparative
freedom to choose how, when and where we shall live and
labour in the Father's Vineyard.   Such teaching reveals the
pre-ordained drama of the human soul, which is epitomized
in the great initiations of Jesus that are hidden in the allegories
of the Gospels, herein unveiled.

CHAPTER II

The first object of this inquiry is to discover whether the Gospel narratives contain something more than an account of the physical life and exoteric teachings of the Prophet of Nazareth. Close examination shows that they conceal some of his innermost spiritual doctrines, and also the secret training which he evidently reserved for and expounded only to his most advanced pupils.

Some portions of the Evangel reveal experiences that are so profound and personal that only an initiate of the highest rank, such as Jesus certainly was, could have so ingeniously recorded them under the veil of the literal text. Certain unique episodes of a superphysical nature are portrayed as though they were simple biographical incidents in his human career, whereas they were divine revelations, celestial blessings, and eternal principles of human life. Only an individual of his exceptional calibre and spiritual attainment could personally have known and described these experiences in such concise and subtle symbolical language. A true symbol tends to conceal its mystery from the ignorant, but reveals it to the wise. Several conspicuous features in his recorded life demonstrate that Jesus was at times utterly alone, such as during his ordeal of temptation in the wilderness and his mental agony in the Garden of Gethsemane. Therefore he was the only person conscious of those abnormal experiences, and the sole witness of the pregnant words that were then presumably uttered. Consequently, no one else but he could have written, or otherwise narrated them. Some events were

7

of so intimate and spiritual a nature that they constitute veritable secrets of the soul, and therefore it would have been little short of sacrilege to speak about them, even to his closest disciples.

Being the founder of Christendom for the Piscean era, his problem was how best to preserve his superphysical experiences and translate them into mystical doctrines for the guidance of posterity. At times his followers seemed to manifest a pathetic lack of vision and spiritual comprehension, which would indicate that they were not then adequately qualified either to understand or to expound his Teaching. Even at the tragic close of his mission, Peter denied that he knew his Master. So how can we assume that, prior to the Crucifixion at least, any of the disciples knew or understood those solemn and sacred experiences that a high initiate must endure, and which figure so conspicuously in his Palestinian career !

The sayings of the Master are remarkably profound and sublime, yet so ingenious and cryptic is their expression that it seems doubtful, if not quite impossible, that his pupils could have memorized them, by single or conjoint effort, merely after having heard them enunciated once. It is almost inconceivable that anyone could remember the essential details of such exalted doctrines, and then transmit them to others, letter perfect, 50 to 100 years after his departure. We have no reliable evidence to prove that any one of his known followers made a written record of his teachings.

It is an anomaly that Christian authorities should confess they do not know who were the real authors of the four Gospels upon which their Faith is founded. The earliest documents extant, which are presumed to be authentic copies or translations of the original records, are the Codex Sinaiticus, now in the British Museum, and the Codex Vaticanus. Both of these are believed to date back no earlier than the 4th century A.D.

Theological scholars acknowledge they do not know who wrote the Second Gospel, for it seems dubious that he was the cousin of Barnabas. Doubt is cast upon the writer of the third Gospel being the physician who travelled at times with Paul, for much is similar to Mark's Gospel. The literary style and skill of the Luke work is superior to that of any of the other evangelists, and it was written in Greek, whereas Aramaic was the language used by Jesus and his followers.

The Gospels recount instances when the disciples made a special request that Jesus should explain some of the symbolical aspects of his parables, which contain only the ethical teaching that he gave openly to the public. This proves that during his lifetime his most advanced pupils were still far from having attained the requisite spiritual illumination which would enable them to comprehend his mystical doctrines, and also to record them in the eloquent phrases of his inspired language.

An analysis of some conspicuous episodes shows that almost every aspect of his Teaching has a double meaning, literal and spiritual. This demonstrates that only high initiates, who were personally familiar with definite celestial visions and mystical experiences, could possibly describe and understand those inner events in the life of Jesus that we find so graphically expressed in the Gospels.

During the past few decades some students, who have made penetrating research into early Christian history, have expressed their conviction that there already existed a unique but obscure manuscript, before any of the Gospels were actually written. This document they denominate the *Quelle*, meaning the Source, which is a very appropriate title. Confirmation that some such writing was extant is furnished by a statement that when Paul first met the Apostles in Jerusalem, a few years after the Crucifixion, they showed him secret manuscripts which were then in their possession. These apparently incorporated some of the innermost doctrines of Jesus, which were known as the Logia of the Master.

Although these documents were revered in sacred remembrance of the Nazarene, Paul was permitted to read them, and he probably copied some extracts therefrom, as he had not known the Master in person.

It is a matter of supreme importance to investigate to what extent Jesus himself might have been the original author, or recorder, of the *Quelle* document, which probably furnished the most intimate and inspiring features of the Gospel stories. It seems evident that some of his spiritual experiences were first recorded in order to represent different stages of progress in the attainment of God-realization.

Many mystics and esoteric students during the past century have expressed the opinion that the Gospel records were specially compiled in order to explain the sequence of superphysical occurrences that an initiate on the spiritual path must endure ere he attains liberation from his earthly pilgrimage. They add that Jesus evidently assumed the rôle of the aspirant.

Apart from the minor initiations that may be given by man in esoteric schools of spiritual training on earth, there are several greater initiations that can only be conferred on superphysical planes by celestial beings. These metaphysical experiences correspond to the five great initiations leading to Masterhood, which stages of progress are delineated in the Gospel stories under the guise of : the Virgin Birth, the Baptism, the Transfiguration, the Crucifixion, Resurrection, and concluded by the Ascension or Reunion with the Father.

An examination of Matthew's story of the birth of Jesus evokes numerous questions that appear unanswerable. It is shrouded in mystery, for it records the intervention of the Holy Spirit and describes various dreams during which the Angel of the Lord gave important instructions to Joseph.

To whom did Joseph recount his remarkable visions whereby they could be so clearly and concisely described ? For example :

" Joseph, thou son of David, fear not to take unto
thee Mary, thy wife, for that which is conceived in
her is of the Holy Ghost."

Then again :

" The Angel of the Lord appeared to Joseph in a
dream, saying, arise and take the young child and
his mother and flee into Egypt."

These were apparently individual experiences that exerted
an emphatic influence in his subsequent life. They were
obviously of such an intimate and unusual nature that they
would most probably have been guarded with the utmost
secrecy. It is generally assumed that Joseph died before
Jesus began his Ministry, consequently he would not have
had personal contact with any of the disciples to whom he
might have recounted the mysterious events that presumably
accompanied the birth of Jesus. There is no record that
Joseph ever spoke concerning the life of his accredited son.
Certainly, if the dream-visions of the Angel of the Lord were
what they purport to be in the literal text, it is conceivable
that he might have revealed them to his wife. But the character of Mary is precisely delineated to show that she was a very
quiet and modest person, who preferred to " ponder these
things in her heart " rather than talk about them.

The angelic interventions accompanying the Nativity have
been generally accepted on their face value, because they tend
to prove the divine origin of Jesus, which should not be
questioned. One may inquire whether such exceptional
features in his infancy were essential in order to demonstrate
that he was the " Only Begotten Son of God," or, as some
zealous advocates affirm, the sole Incarnation of the Deity
Himself ?

A similar question might be applied to the journey of the
erstwhile magi, and other supernormal happenings in relation
to the birth of Jesus. There is no assurance that the three

wise men recounted their individual experiences to anyone else, for they were explicitly instructed by the Lord to return to their own abode in the East by a different route, in order to avoid meeting Herod in Jerusalem. Thus it is written :

> " After they had seen the young child, with Mary
> his Mother, and being warned of God in a dream,
> they departed into their own country another way."

If the magi were truly wise men, why should they have talked about a sacred vision that had apparently been vouch-safed only to them, especially when they had an extraordinary star to guide them during their long journey ? They were thereby the indirect cause of Herod's anger, and the subsequent massacre of the innocents, that unpardonable murder of :

> " all the children that were in Bethlehem, from two
> years old and under, according to the time which
> he had diligently inquired of the wise men."

Could such a tragedy have been a worthy precedent to the coming of the Messiah ? Such an incongruous sequence of abnormal events does not help to convince the mind of earnest seekers for Truth, or kindle the hearts of the lovers of God. Can we believe that the life of the Messiah and Saviour of mankind was heralded by the inconsolable anguish of so many heart-broken parents, caused by such a heinous crime ? Surely, when faced with such problems, we are *not* justified in accepting or adhering to the literal text of the Scriptures when it bespeaks so much unnecessary human sorrow. Rather we should obey the behest of the Master and seek the spirit underlying the letter. If we search for the deeper esoteric and mystical interpretation, we shall find all these difficulties will disappear in a flood of illuminating revelation, which will enlighten the mind, give solace to the heart and lead to the liberation of the soul.

If we attempt to interpret the nativity story of Jesus as a covert illustration of the mystical second birth, so strongly advocated by him, we shall be able to elucidate the profound significance of that remarkable event.   In a similar manner, if we apply an esoteric interpretation to other mysteries pertaining to the life of the Master, we shall realize that instead of destroying our faith, such investigation will give it a far more rational basis and undeniable justification.

CHAPTER III

The real purpose of religion is to point out the way whereby man may regain conscious union with the Father. A Sacred Scripture reflects the teaching that one of the messengers of God brought to the world. Therefore, the underlying spirit of the Gospels should reveal the nature of the soul, and give mystical tuition showing how one may travel safely on the Path of Return.

The narrative " according to St. Mathew " describes this spiritual journey as made by the Essene initiate Jesus, who subsequently became our leader and spiritual guide. A record is given of the path he trod, the difficulties he encountered and the triumphal success he accomplished. These steps designate the inner life, or Drama of the Soul, in which each one of us must eventually play the principal rôle, hence our need to understand its salient features.

It is significant that in the first 17 verses of this Gospel the obscure author seeks to trace the genealogy of Jesus, first from Abraham down to David, then to the captivity of the Israelites in Babylon, and finally to Joseph the husband of Mary. Why should the writer emphasize three phases of 14 generations, and give the lineage of 42 ancestors of Jesus ? It may be inferred that he wished to impress the Jews, but had he another objective ? According to Bible chronology Abraham began his mission in the year 1921 B.C. when he was 75 years of age. As a generation from father to son usually corresponds to 25 years, the period from the birth of Abraham to that of Jesus might have embraced 80 generations, instead of merely 42.

Again, what was the purpose of selecting divisions so unequal in extent ? From Abraham to David, who was presumably born in 1078 B.C., would give a total of 918 years, and allow for 37 generations, whereas only 14 are recorded. Yet from the birth of David to the " carrying away into Babylon " in 606 B.C. leaves an interim of only 312 years, a more proportionate time for the 2nd series of 13 or 14 generations. The third section is measured from the Babylonian captivity to the birth of Jesus in 4 B.C., giving a period of 602 years that might account for 24 generations !

A synopsis of the cypher number from 1 to 10, with the symbolic meanings that Moses and the Hebrew prophets attached to them, will clarify the foregoing :

Number 1 : Suggests God, the One, the Beginning, Immutable stability, and all Divine attributes.

Number 2 : Implies ideas of mutation, change and transition from one state to another, and of relative duration and growth ; it is a symbol of duality, and therefore is the opposite of everything indicated by number 1. It suggests all that is human, but not Divine.

Number 3 : Contains the opposed ideas of the first two numbers, and it may be combined into a relative unit as cypher 3, then it indicates liberation, eternal happiness and peace ; it symbolizes the ideal union of divine and human qualities in earthly life.

Number 4 : Conveys the idea of strength, solidity and grandeur, also the greatness which results from numerical addition and multiplication of its units, i.e., 1, 2, 3 and 4.

Number 5 : Indicates human comprehension through the exercise of the five external senses ; therefore this cypher represents Man or Woman.

Number 6 :   Signifies equality, equilibrium and due fitness of conditions. It represents proportional measurement leading to the higher accomplishment as indicated in number 7.

Number 7 :   Means the consummation of things and times, the completion of a cycle and return to the Source ; it also represents the septenary nature of man and all the cosmos.

Number 8 :   Springs from a double root and suggests accumulation, augmentation, and placing one thing upon another, such as the higher self being elevated on the basis of the lower self of man.

Number 9 :   Gives the notion of restoration, consolidation and conservation of things or qualities.

Number 10 :   Designates aggregation, the power to govern and direct ; it also symbolizes the Father-Mother-Deity.

The esoteric or cypher meaning of these numbers is found by the addition of the digits, thus 234 = 9, and means " restoration and conservation." So the assumed age of Methuselah of 969 years first represents 24 and finally the cypher 6, thus indicating the presage of final accomplishment indicated in the number 7.

Similar import may have been applied to the numbers employed in this Gospel, with a special, though hidden, purpose. The digits of 14 summarize into the cypher 5, which symbolizes man. It may therefore be assumed that the primary period of 14 generations is an indication that those persons who seek union with the Father must first develop the masculine qualities of physical courage, moral integrity and sound intelligence. Then, as the cypher 5 also pertains to woman, the second period of 14 generations would represent the development of traditional feminine faculties, such as patient endurance, maternal love and intuition. The final

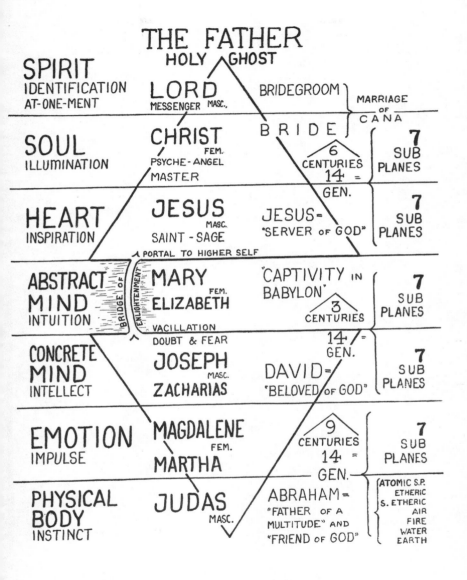

THE FATHER
HOLY GHOST

SPIRIT
IDENTIFICATION
AT-ONE-MENT

LORD
MESSENGER MASC.,

BRIDEGROOM

MARRIAGE
OF
CANA

SOUL
ILLUMINATION

CHRIST
FEM.
PSYCHE - ANGEL
MASTER

B R I D E

6 CENTURIES
14 = GEN.

7 SUB PLANES

HEART
INSPIRATION

JESUS
MASC.
SAINT - SAGE

JESUS = "SERVER OF GOD"

7 SUB PLANES

A PORTAL TO HIGHER SELF

ABSTRACT MIND
INTUITION

BRIDGE OF
ENLIGHTENMENT

MARY
FEM.
ELIZABETH
VACILLATION

"CAPTIVITY IN BABYLON"

3 CENTURIES

7 SUB PLANES

CONCRETE MIND
INTELLECT

DOUBT & FEAR

JOSEPH
MASC.
ZACHARIAS

14 / GEN.

DAVID = "BELOVED OF GOD"

7 SUB PLANES

EMOTION
IMPULSE

MAGDALENE
FEM.

MARTHA

9 CENTURIES
14 = GEN.

7 SUB PLANES

PHYSICAL BODY
INSTINCT

JUDAS
MASC.

ABRAHAM = "FATHER OF A MULTITUDE" AND "FRIEND OF GOD"

ATOMIC S.P.
ETHERIC
S. ETHERIC
AIR
FIRE
WATER
EARTH

period of 14 generations suggests the ultimate series of lives of the initiate, who must blend into a harmonious combination these dual characteristics, that is the positive or masculine with the responsive or feminine. Their perfect mastery then finds expression in nobility of character, wise discrimination and universal love, for these characterize the perfect man, personified as Jesus.

This cumulative inference suggests that the author of Matthew sought to demonstrate the progressive steps of development of the human soul in general. The inner life of Jesus was presented as the best example of perfected man, because he summarized all his previous stages of unfoldment and completed his human evolution as the Prophet of Nazareth.

These subtle ideas find confirmation in the opening 17 verses of this first chapter. The summation of these digits makes 8, and the corresponding cypher indicates the building up of faculties related to the higher self, of which the soul is the apex. It is the inner source of guidance and the stimulus to every effort that is evoked by purified desire, selfless devotion and spiritual aspiration.

The triple repetition of 14 generations introduces the cypher 3, which combines the divine attributes that are signified by number 1, added to the 2 characteristics of the physical and spiritual nature of man, who is an embodiment of human and divine qualities. These basic ideals are ingeniously veiled, but constitute an appropriate preamble to the record of spiritual progress of the initiate, who is personified in the life of the Nazarene.

There may also be a profound purpose implied by repeating the number 14 three times, for this corresponds to 6 periods of 7. Esoteric students know there are 7 major planes comprising human nature, each plane having 7 subdivisions. These suggest the recurrent incarnations and steps of progress that man makes in the final course of his evolution.

At first the aspirant is personified as Abraham, the meaning of this name being : " Father of a multitude," which indicates the need of lengthy and diverse experiences. In the accompanying chart the planes are described alternately as masculine and feminine, and recurrent incarnations on each duad would give equilibrium in the three series of 14 generations. On its journey the soul lives in many different bodies in order to embrace all possible human experiences. However, there often ensues a period of oscillation when crossing the bridge of enlightenment. This is most aptly described as Captivity in Babylon, because there is invariably some confusion in the mind of the neophyte as to whether he is right or wise in taking such a step. When he reaches the plane of concrete intellect, and is well equipped with worldly knowledge, he is represented as Joseph, the seeker who begins his quest for Light on the Path.

Investigation into the Hebrew meanings of the principal names mentioned in this Gospel furnishes another clue to solve these mysteries. Abram was the original name of the prophet before he received his initiation from the Angel of the Lord ; this name means : " Father of exaltation," designating an advanced initiate. Then, by the incorporation of the letters " ha," implying influx of divine breath, his name was changed to Abraham in order to denote his mission as the " Father of a multitude." He is the acknowledged founder of the Hebrew nation, to whom he brought the ideal of monotheism, the message of faith in the One Living God. His recorded life describes in metaphor the progressive stages of spiritual development. The mystical title ascribed to Abraham by the Semitic people is : " the Friend of God." This corresponds to man's first major step towards reaching Christhood and spiritual liberation, which is portrayed as the recurrent ideal throughout the Bible. When the seeker begins to traverse the path of return, he must bring into the consciousness of the personality the realization that God is

verily the Father of all mankind.   He is the most trustworthy
Friend we have, for upon Him we may call whenever we are in
need, because His sympathy and support are universal and
assured.

After tracing the 14 generations of Abraham's descendants,
the ancestral record of Jesus gives emphasis to the name
David, which means : " Beloved of God."   This signifies the
second stage in man's spiritual unfoldment.   It infers that the
candidate has progressed sufficiently for God to meet him on
the way and accept him as one of His beloved children.   It is
stated that David was the son of Jesse, a Hebrew name
implying that : " The Creative Deity really exists," the
assumption being that he recognized the Presence of God.
The exoteric meaning of the name Jesse is : " firm and
upright ; " these are the requisite qualities that an aspirant
must first develop.   It is recorded that Jesse was a " Bethlehemite," but the implication of this title is that he sought
spiritual sustenance in the " house of bread," for Bethlehem
designates a secret school of esoteric training and spiritual
sustenance.

As the direct inheritor of these attributes David was anointed
King of Israel, in substitution of Saul who was dethroned
because he was an embodiment of egoism and petulant
disobedience.   The centre of rulership in an individual must
be gradually transferred from the head, symbolizing concrete
intellect and personal will, to the heart, centre of devotion to
God, by doing His Will in selfless service to one's neighbour.
Prior to his kingship David manifested similar qualities to
those ascribed to Orpheus, because by means of the wonderful
music he produced on his harp, signifying his own heart, he
often soothed the angry moods and irate nature of Saul.   In
those early days of his life David communed daily with God
in prayer and meditation.   That was the training he received
from Samuel, a highly evolved spiritual leader and head of the
esoteric school of ancient mystery teaching in Israel, David

being his most advanced pupil. This finds confirmation in the statement that : " David was born in Bethlehem," a synonym indicating a sanctuary of spiritual tuition, for it does not simply mean the village of that name.

An analysis of Matthew's genealogy of Jesus discloses almost complete disagreement with the ancestors recorded in the Luke Gospel. Matthew's list is traced through Solomon, the royal successor of David, whereas the Luke lineage is derived from his son Nathan. Both acknowledge the paternity of Joseph and revert to David, thus fulfilling the prophecies regarding the Messiah. It is significant that whereas the first Gospel records only 41 ancestors, the third gives 54 names, a divergence that creates a perplexing problem. This may be understood if we perceive that Matthew's narrative was expressed in simile and symbol, and has profound mystical meanings hidden under the literal text.

By applying an esoteric key we find it offers a rational solution to this paradox. The inconsistencies above cited demonstrate that the author did not wish his genealogy to be taken altogether literally. Rather, it seems he employed it to show he was not only dealing with the life of a single individual, but also with human souls in their course of spiritual evolution. In this narrative Jesus fills the rôle of a pioneer who has gone ahead on the mystical path, to open the way for those who are ready to take up their cross and follow him.

The recorded list of his ancestors may quite appropriately symbolize the previous incarnations of a candidate for initiation, for many of the names have special meanings that correspond to various stages of higher development. For example :

Booz (Boaz) signifies : " cheerful willingness," and suggests an innate zeal in the quest of Truth.

David   means : " well beloved."

Solomon   implies : " peace and concord."

Josophat	indicates : " unfolding the ideal of Godhead," which a candidate must ultimately do.
Joram	suggests : " whom Jehovah has exalted."
Ezekias	designates : " the power of the Lord to restore the temple," man's spiritual abode not made with hands.
Josias	denotes : " whom Jehovah heals."
Zorobabel	means : " dispersion of illusion," which is an essential precedent to initiation.
Eliakim	signifies : " whom God has established," and points to a definite state of advancement.
Sadoc	indicates : " one who is upright and venerated."
Eleazar	denotes : " God is the helper," and every initiate realizes this is true.
Joseph	signifies : " He shall increase progressively," and is the most significant name of all.

Applying these Hebrew interpretations to the presumed earlier lives of the candidate, we perceive that they constitute a very rational preparation for one who wishes to undertake the quest for God-consciousness.

It is to be noted that in V. 17 of this text the conspicuous feature of " carrying away into Babylon " is inserted as the nominal division between the second and third series of 14 generations, and actually is regarded as an ancestor. This is very significant, because the word Babylon is a Greek derivative of the Hebrew " Babel " and means " confusion and chaos." Therefore, to be captive in such a condition implies that state of transition when the range of understanding is becoming expanded and the seeker realizes that worldly knowledge acquired by the concrete intellect is not an adequate basis to guide one on the Spiritual Path. Previous to attaining the innate wisdom transmitted through the faculty of intuition the aspirant tends to oscillate between the objective and subjective planes, and to feel a sense of instability and confusion. This disappears as he passes onwards and upwards, and crosses over from the limited knowledge of mundane existence, which proves to be illusory, and eventually attains the sagacity of an idealist, who reflects divine Wisdom. Thus the captivity in Babylon is an eloquent analogy for that state of doubt and hesitation which was ascribed to Joseph before he would accept Mary as his " wife." He represents the state of consciousness centred in the intellect and imprisoned in the personality, whereas she symbolizes its subsequent elevation into the more expanded range of intuition in the individuality. Therefore the candidate for these mysteries must have confidence in his inner guidance. When his intuition begins to function he must be ready to accept it as the guiding principle of his life, for worldly standards will no longer satisfy the spiritual urge which now impels him forward. Only thus can he liberate his soul from bondage.

These aspects are presented so adroitly that they may be passed over unperceived, but from the foregoing analysis one can discern that underlying the prologue to this Gospel there are concealed the preliminary steps which the aspirant must take on the Path to Reunion. These stages are symbolically disguised as ancestors of Jesus because they necessarily preceded the fuller expression of Christhood in his manifestation as the promised Messiah to the people of Israel. Jesus is a Greek name derived from the Hebrew Jeshua, and means : " whose help Jehovah is," or : " deliverance through God," and thence it also implies " saviour " of men. He was the ideal " Son of Man," though his esoteric title was : " Server of God." This state subsequently led on to the higher degree of becoming the Christ, or " Son of God," whence he was ultimately elevated to the sublime rank of " The Lord," being " At-one with God."

It is of paramount importance that students of esoteric Christianity should recognize these progressive stages of development as disclosed in Matthew's biography of the prophet of Nazareth. In this manner it can be better understood how he accomplished the mission which qualified him to become our Spiritual Guide and Redeemer. Whereas we may be only now entering the Path, he traversed the whole journey and found God awaiting him with the welcome : " Well done, thou good and faithful servant ; enter thou into the glory of thy Lord." Only when Jesus had completed this great spiritual adventure, and had achieved his pre-ordained destiny by raising his manhood into the Godhead, could he effectively assist his brethren on earth. Then in fact he sacrificed his well-earned bliss of the Father's Abode, and " descended from Heaven," to be an Avatar, or embodiment of God-consciousness, as the Way, the Life and the Truth for mankind to follow.

He zealously sought to give spiritual teaching to the world, to explain his innermost experiences, and so enable every aspiring seeker to adopt the most efficacious means of liberating his soul from material bondage and further incarnations on earth. This accomplishment has been variously described in Christianity as : Redemption, Salvation and Reunion with the Father, although these really depict the three final stages of mystical attainment. This consummation can only be achieved by gradual development of latent faculties bequeathed by God to every soul when it was first endowed with individual consciousness. Since that time in remote antiquity it has had innumerable experiences in a series of physical bodies. This has extended over an immeasurable period of time, and has involved repeated lives in diverse epochs and races, possibly in alternating male and female bodies, so that the soul may acquire the utmost knowledge possible under all planetary conditions and zodiacal vicissitudes.

Only in the final phases of these earthly experiences do the higher faculties of the individual become awakened. The soul is then partially released from its most dense coverings, and begins to assert its innate spiritual hunger. Gradually it is able to manifest its true nature, and reveal the divine mission and creative activity it is destined to fulfil. Every soul is like an independent instrument in a mighty orchestra, therefore it must play its own music in the divine Symphony, under the direction of the Master Musician. Seven successive stages of superphysical evolution, and man's corresponding progress on the path to God realization, are unveiled in the Gospel stories, under the following titles :

1 :   The Mystical Virgin Birth, or spiritual regeneration into the realm of the higher self, and thence on to the state of Jesushood.

2 :   The Baptism and benediction of the Holy Spirit, with the subsequent attainment of Christhood.

3 :   The Temptation in the wilderness, being the final test and subjugation of the egocentric personality.

4 :   The Transfiguration on the Mount, a vision revealing the immortal nature of the soul and its entry into the " Kingdom of Heaven," which was supplemented by the " Marriage in Cana."

5 :   The " Winepress " of Gethsemane, the liberation from bondage of self hood ; " may Thy Will be done."

6 :   The Crucifixion at Golgotha or the " passing over " and final surrender of the limited individual soul unto the Universal Being.

7 :   The Resurrection or realization of the divine nature of the human spirit, and the Ascension or At-one-ment, being the final merging of the manhood into the Godhead.

Each one of these degrees marks a crucial scene in the Drama of the Soul. They are summarized in the mystical life of Jesus Christ in order to reveal to the inner vision and understanding of the aspirant his future course of progress, before he can reach the glorious apotheosis of human destiny and attain reunion with the Father.

As this is the greatest enterprise man can ever undertake, it should be approached with courage, discerning discrimination, and without bias or prejudice. If we could read between the lines of the original text of Genesis and the Gospels, we should find the true spirit that giveth life, and not only discover a logical appeal to satisfy the reason, but also that which awakens intuitive insight and kindles the heart with gladness. The Christ Doctrines reveal spiritual light that illuminates the soul with irrefutable perception of divine Truth, and guides it on the path to the final goal of human attainment.

CHAPTER IV

MYSTICAL SIGNIFICANCE OF THE NATIVITY STORY

An esoteric study of the recorded life of Jesus Christ reveals that, apart from its biographical aspect, the outstanding events and experiences portray a mystical allegory representing the journey of the human soul towards God-realization. This does not imply that the Master, his parents and disciples were not living people, but it does suggest that their individual characters were purposely delineated in a particular manner in order to demonstrate the specific nature of certain stages in man's spiritual progress on the Path of Attainment.

The Gospel stories are of perennial interest, and constitute an irresistible appeal, because every individual is travelling along the same highway until reunion with the Father shall be accomplished. Every person receives a constant, though silent, urge to undertake this spiritual quest, because it is the essence of God's Creative Plan for mankind. Therefore an endeavour to understand this inner mystery of life gives to earnest seekers a constantly increasing joy and deeper enthusiasm, as they approach more closely to His Abode.

In v. 16 of the first chapter, the writer of Matthew introduces four principal characters, with a special objective which becomes more self-evident when analysed in detail. The unknown author must have been the Master himself, for only one who had passed through such transcendental experiences could describe them in the subtle and symbolic language that has been bequeathed to posterity. Although the nativity story is preceded by the assumed ancestors of Joseph, rather than those of Mary, and should rationally lead up to Jesus, emphasis is given to him " who is called Christ." This word means " an anointed one," Christhood being the spiritual Office attained by Jesus. It is a state of development that can be achieved by all zealous seekers, as Paul clearly affirmed. The text reads :

" Jacob begat Joseph the husband of Mary, of whom was born Jesus, who is called Christ."

The reason for this sequence of characters is that the fundamental theme of the Gospels is the predestined unfoldment of the Christhood faculty that is inherent in all mankind. The author proceeds to expound this in simile and allegory, though under the guise of one exemplary individual, who is the ideal model for all his followers.

" Now the birth of Jesus Christ was on this wise : when as his mother Mary was espoused to Joseph, before they came together, she was found with child of the Holy Ghost.
" Then Joseph her husband, being a just man, and not willing to make her a public example, was minded to put her away privily.
" But while he thought on these things, behold the Angel of the Lord appeared unto him in a dream, saying, Joseph, thou son of David, fear not to take unto thee Mary thy wife ; for that which is conceived in her is of the Holy Ghost."

Although this may appear to be a naïve statement of a human biological event, it is veiled under such abnormal conditions that it is raised to a metaphysical plane. Esoteric analysis reveals that it is a true allegory, a fiction with a meaning beyond the literal. Mgr. Ronald Knox translates the last sentence of v. 20 thus :

" For it is by the power of the Holy Ghost that she has conceived this child."

This is obviously more mystical. It is, in fact, a carefully designed description of the mystical conception that must precede the second birth, which Jesus so emphatically taught to those who sought the spiritual way of life. Therefore it was quite appropriate to introduce it at the beginning of the New Testament.

Apart from his ethical teaching in the Sermons and Parables, the emphatic injunction of the Master to Nicodemus : " Ye must be born again," remains the most conspicuous but abstruse feature of the Christ Doctrines. In fact, he affirmed it was the essential precedent even to " see the Kingdom of Heaven." Consequently, it is of supreme importance that we should strive to understand its deeper meaning, and if we can penetrate behind the letter of the text we shall discover its profound spiritual significance.

Intuitive perception shows that the character of Joseph was delineated to represent the *objective mind* of the candidate who is seeking initiation into the sacred mysteries of life, and the description of him as " a just man " indicates that he was an earnest aspirant. But his unenlightened intellect was not willing, nor even able to recognize the dawning faculty of his latent *feminine intuition*, which is here designated as Mary. Although it is declared : " they were espoused," meaning they were destined to be united, " they had not yet come together," nevertheless she had already " conceived." This statement definitely implies that, whereas the concrete lower mind and the abstract higher mind can be exercised independently, they must eventually work in conjunction and in harmony. The primary purpose of the intuition is to form a bridge to join the lower self of the personality with the higher self of the individuality. This is the first essential step towards that true enlightenment which comes from within " to lighten every man that cometh into the world."

The most sublime vehicle of consciousness is the human Spirit, for it receives and reflects the divine attributes of

Living Light. As the supernal nature of the aspirant is gradually awakened and expanded, his directive will becomes correspondingly stronger, and he grows more zealous and one-pointed. Then, as he elevates the centre of his consciousness, there is a reciprocal action by the descent of the divine Spirit working through the soul. Eventually this impregnates his heart with the germ of spiritual light, engendering the conscious activity of impersonal love which is personified as Jesus. The responsiveness between the yearning aspiration of man and the benediction of God is figuratively expressed as the generative power of the Holy Spirit, which causes the mystical conception. Such mutual co-operation brings into being the " Holy Child " whose subsequent inner birth is truly virginal, because it is undefiled in its nature and divine in its origin.

This mystical conception and virginal birth are purposely presented under the guise of abnormal physical events in order to demonstrate the requisite human foundation for our superstructure. It will be recognized that the three-dimensional man, with his limited concrete intellect, can only understand empirical proof of physical facts and phenomena. Therefore it is correct to state that Joseph was not the paternal source of Jesushood in the higher self, nor of the awakening of the soul consciousness, which corresponds to the Christhood. This incapacity of the lower mind is aptly described : " Joseph being minded to put her away privily."

Very often the normal worldly man is ashamed to acknowledge that he sometimes feels an inner urge towards higher ideals, and senses an intuitive perception of something which, although apparently illogical and inscrutable, yet is obviously true. To some people an inner voice is audible, and this corresponds to the " Angel of the Lord " saying : " fear not," for the Angel symbolizes the soul receiving light on the Path, from the Lord or Guiding Spirit within.

With the further and irresistible quickening of this consciousness, the earnest aspirant does take courage, and he responds to inner guidance with increasing confidence. This entrancing state, though thinly veiled to the understanding of the seeker, is beautifully explained in :

> " She shall bring forth a son, and thou shalt call his name Jesus, for he shall save his people from their sins."

This is indeed a remarkable statement. In a mystical sense, to the candidate for higher initiation, Jesus represents the embodiment of impersonal and expanding love, whereas " his people " signify the lower self and its perverse propensities, which must be henceforth restrained and their effects sublimated, that is, " saved," redeemed and brought back to their pristine purity and primordial state of Paradise.

During the earlier development of the egocentric personality it assumed the right to satisfy its instinctive desires, without giving consideration or sympathy to the welfare of others. It is therefore evident that many are responsible for past sins of commission and omission. These constitute *bad karma*, the debit items in spiritual accountancy which must eventually be liquidated " to the uttermost farthing." This process of redemption may be partially accomplished by a reverse action of generous giving, and by rendering kindly service for the benefit of others, without consideration of reward or recognition.

> " All this was done that it might be fulfilled which was spoken of the Lord by the prophet, saying behold a virgin shall be with child and shall bring forth a son, and thou shalt call his name Emmanual, meaning God is with us."

This quotation merits elucidation in order to verify what was the real intent of the Prophet in expressing such significant words, and also to discover the reason why they are incorporated in this Gospel. There is no evidence to prove that this statement in Isaiah, VIII, 14, was intended to serve as a prophecy regarding the birth of Jesus, which only occurred about 740 years later. The context of this quotation actually describes a local historical episode. An act of aggressive warfare was being launched by Rezin, king of Syria, in connivance with Pekah, prince of Israel, against Jerusalem, which was in charge of Prince Ahaz.

Despite the geographical aspect of this story, its mystical significance is far more important than any transient event of Palestinian history. The veil covering this mystery resides in the meanings of the Hebrew names recorded. Prince Ahaz was the son of Jotham, which designates : " he whom the Lord makes perfect." Ahaz signifies : " the possessor or guardian," and Jerusalem the : " vision or state of peace," which he was defending. By contrast, we are told that the Holy City was being besieged by two assailants, whom the Lord, speaking through the prophet, describes as : " the two tails of these smoking fire-brands." The purport of the names of these enemies adds to their sinister significance, for Rezin is interpreted as : " wicked pleasure and wantonness," while Pekah appropriately implies : " a conspirator, and one who is watchful in taking advantage of the weakness of another person." Further, it is said he was the son of Remaliah, or : " spiritual pride," a very apt allusion.

The gist of this story is that Ahaz, being a prince, is really an initiate on the spiritual path, and upon him is imposed the task of protecting the city of peace, which is his soul, from the insidious attacks of the egoistic lower self. At first his efforts are frustrated by powerful enemies, for Rezin represents the emotional impulses, while Pekah indicates self-satisfaction and intellectual pride, with its confidence in knowledge of worldly affairs, but which does not understand the spiritual nature of that *inner peace* implied by the name Jerusalem.

Ahaz is very depressed, and in his despair he turns to the prophet for counsel :

" Then said the Lord unto Isaiah, say unto him,
take heed and be quiet; fear not, neither be faint-
hearted because they say let us make a bridge and
set up a king in Judah. Thus saith the Lord God :
It shall not stand, neither shall it come to pass."

In a mystical sense the lower self is not permitted to persist
in dominating the soul. As Ahaz still expressed human
frailty and doubt, the Lord spoke again :

" If ye will not believe, surely ye shall not be established ; "

that is, in the state of inner peace of Jerusalem, the soul.

" Ask thee a sign of the Lord Thy God, ask it either
in the depth or in the height above."

Happily, Ahaz revealed the requisite qualities of an initiate by
his modesty and restraint, saying : " I will not ask, neither
will I tempt the Lord."   Then Isaiah replied :

" Hear ye now, O house of David ; is it a small thing
for you to weary my God ? Therefore the Lord
Himself shall give you a sign ; *behold a virgin shall
conceive, and bear a son, and shall call his name
Immanuel.* Butter and honey shall he eat that he
may know how to refuse the evil and choose the
good.   But before the child shall know how to refuse
the evil and choose the good, the land that thou
abhorest shall be forsaken by both her kings."

Although the above may appear to be an abstruse synopsis
of the situation, it is really a succinct metaphorical description
of the tests and difficulties the aspirant encounters in his quest
for spiritual Truth.   It also proves how necessary is it to have
the guidance of an Elder Brother on the Path.   The full
meaning of the word *virgin* is defined as, not only a *chaste
maiden*, but also an *unsullied youth*. Both are appropriate
synonyms indicating the nature of the soul, which in its essence
is divine, therefore ever pure and virgin.

The primary question is whether Isaiah was narrating a local episode, or making a subtle reference to the mystical second birth within the heart of his pupil and initiate, Ahaz. The accepted rôle of a prophet is to be a spiritual guide to those who seek God-realization, therefore he must deal more with eternal and mystical matters than with simple physical affairs of human life.

As the meaning of Jerusalem is : " city of peace, a peaceful abode, or the vision of peace," it is obviously an apt simile for the soul, which was placed under the conscious care of Ahaz, the aspiring initiate.   It should be noted that he was addressed as : " O house of David," a title similar to that applied to Joseph : " thou son of David."   Both David and Jesus were said to be " born in Bethlehem," the inference being that they both received esoteric instruction and training in that secret school of mystery teaching.

The curious phrase : " butter and honey shall he eat," is quite in keeping with these ideas, for whereas cream is the best part of milk, the food for babes or young pupils, butter is the transmutation of cream, and is an appropriate analogy for the deeper wisdom acquired by higher initiates.   In a similar manner honey represents the essence of flowers in nature, the manuscript of God, for upon His works should the aspirant muse in order to understand the deeper mysteries of life.

Deep tuition and careful discipline of the candidate prepare him with knowledge and courage to : " refuse the evil and choose the good."   However, before this final qualification is attained there is the imposition : " the land which thou abhorest shall be forsaken of both her kings."   An esoteric interpretation suggests that the " land " which is now disdained by the initiate is the lower self of the personality, whose demands of emotional impulse and egoistic arrogance must first be subordinated before he can proceed further in spiritual development.

Why should the author of Matthew's Gospel have introduced this Isaiah story of " virgin birth " in the opening chapter of the New Testament, unless it was to emphasize that he was also expounding the same subject ? One fact appears irrefutable : that the prophet was fully cognizant of its mystical nature about 750 years before the time of Jesus. This is confirmed by his trenchant remark to Nicodemus when the latter asked : " how can a man be born again when he is old ? " to which Jesus replied : " art thou a *master of Israel* and knowest not these things ? "

Its true significance was also well known in the Orient, where such a degree of spiritual advancement merited the title of " a twice-born." Another important feature to be noted is that although Isaiah specifically states that the " son of the virgin shall be called Immanuel," which Matthew quotes, he also gives the meaning of *Emmanuel* as : " God is with us." Thereby the writer reveals his own understanding that this is a state of spiritual development wherein the initiate realizes the divine Presence within the heart. This was the attainment sought by the early followers of Jesus, and in this manner it is true that he came to fulfil the Mosaic Law and the inner teaching of the prophets.

> " Then Joseph, being raised from sleep, did as the Angel of the Lord had bidden him, and took unto him his wife ; and knew her not till she had brought forth her first born son : and he called his name Jesus."

Joseph assumes the prerogative of the father by giving to Mary's son the name Jesus, but not Immanuel, which obviously proves that the Matthew story was not intended to fulfil the alleged prophecy of Isaiah. The statement : " Joseph being raised from sleep," is an acknowledgement that the writer of this Gospel did not wish to imply that he was awakened from his night's repose. Rather, it suggests that

Joseph had then definitely unfolded a degree of spiritual consciousness pertaining to that more elevated realm which enabled him to realize and also exercise his intuition. Actually it was this new faculty, personified as Mary, that made him aware of the undeniable existence of his own higher self. A person is metaphorically " asleep " until he awakens to the reality of celestial planes of being. While we are normally awake and conscious in this lower physical plane, we are unaware of, and thus asleep to, the existence of spiritual realms. In actual sleep our consciousness can be raised to heavenly spheres, and so we can perceive in vision the Angel of the Lord, who then reveals things that it is not lawful to speak about, being too sublime.

Christian tradition affirms that the parents of Jesus were closely related, and that Joseph was much older than Mary. These ideas are perfectly amenable to an esoteric analysis. Not only is the intellect " closely related " to the intuition of an aspirant, but also, in the psychological process, the concrete lower mind is invariably developed and exercised two or three decades before the abstract higher mind begins to function freely.

Joseph, as the seeker, could only understand his feminine quality of intuition, Mary, when his still higher centre of the " heart " consciousness was born, and when the Holy Child, referred to as Jesus, found expression in utter devotion to God and selfless service to mankind.

This mystical second birth, disguised under the nativity story of Jesus, reflects the first of the great initiations, those inner experiences which the aspirant realizes on the Path to God, and which constitute the essence of the Christ Doctrines.

CHAPTER V

THE BIRTH OF JESUS

This esoteric interpretation reveals that what appears to be biographical, geographical or historical, merely constitutes the framework for priceless jewels of spiritual truth that are encased therein. It is these latter which are all important, being the spirit that underlies the letter of the text.

Chapter II of Matthew's Gospel appropriately describes the second scene in this immortal Drama of the Soul. The first verse is a remarkable example of dramatic and symbolic art, because it expresses many ideas of profound significance, but with such naïve simplicity and brevity that their deeper import is often passed over unperceived. We read :

" When Jesus was born in Bethlehem of Judea, in the days of Herod the king."

Jesus personifies the candidate who is seeking a high initiation in the esoteric school situated in, and therefore denominated as Bethlehem. This name implies : " spiritual sustenance," which was given there, together with the primary degrees of initiation. Such a school had been in existence for many centuries before the birth of Jesus.

Practically all Hebrew names have a deeper significance than is apparent, and the illumined writers of the Bible stories often employed them in order to convey certain ideas that remain hidden until research discloses their true meaning. " Bethlehem of Judea " implies a sanctuary of mystical tuition whose main ideal was to give praise and service to the Lord. " In the days of Herod the King " is a subtle inference that there were then living many students who undertook that course of spiritual training, despite the fact that base materialism dominated the life of most people. Herod designates an earthly ruler who is narrow, jealous and destructive; thereby he impeded the spiritual development of many people. Candidates for the mysteries learn to live the " inner life " and remain detached, although others around them may be caught in the maelstrom of egoism and become involved in the quest for power and position at any price. Dispassion is the first test that the novice must undergo, in order to prove his steadfast worthiness and loyalty to the ideals he wishes to adopt for his life conduct.

This feature is clearly portrayed in the subsequent text : " There came from the East to Jerusalem Wise Men." This is a succinct statement that appears to combine historical and geographical references, whereas its main intent is spiritual. " From the East " is a well-known phrase meaning : " coming from the Orient," the " source of Light," or, the " rising Sun," and the " Dawn of a new Day ; "all these designate the plane of illumination that corresponds to the awakened soul. Hence we may understand that these Wise Men were adepts who had already elevated their consciousness to the higher self, and had passed the heart plane, which for the present is personified as Jesus, whom they wished to help. That they came to Jerusalem suggests they were seeking the " abode of peace," and this confirms that they had realized the spiritual nature of their own souls, and now sought the higher realm corresponding to the Holy Spirit, which is both human and divine, being the link between man and God.

It is feasible that their assumed journey from the East is a covert indication that they were the senior teachers of the chief esoteric school in the Middle East, which was at one time located in Heliopolis in northern Egypt. If so, then it is evident that they had come to Bethlehem to confer a higher initiation upon Jesus, who was their most advanced pupil in

Palestine. These Wise Men could perceive his perfect
purity of life and character, and also his innate capacity to
attain the highest degree of human perfection, the corresponding title for this being appropriately given as " King of the
Jews."

To " see his star in the East " confirms this assumption,
because, as a true initiate progresses on the Path of spiritual
attainment, he becomes more and more illuminated with divine
wisdom.   There is a corresponding increase of light emanating
from the centre within his heart, and this is visible to the inner
vision of the sage and master, even from a distance.   The soul
itself is filled with divine light, and this makes it the font of
true illumination.   Its grade of intensity is the index that
reveals to the master, or spiritual guide, the actual stage of
advancement reached by his pupil.   This being so it is obvious
that one cannot deceive God nor His appointed ministers.
Herod tried to delude the Wise Men, but failed ignominiously.
Therefore the aspirant prays : " Let the star of divine Light,
shining in Thy heart, be reflected in the hearts of Thy de-
votees."

This scene of his inner life depicts Jesus as the young initiate
who is reaching the stage of the mystical birth, not as an infant
child, but as a mature man.   This state evokes the faculties of
the higher self, comprising the intuition of the abstract mind,
the inspiration of the kindled heart, and the illumination of the
awakened soul.   Although Jesus was already a high initiate at
birth, it was necessary to recapitulate this unfoldment of inner
faculties.

The purpose of the first chapter of this Gospel was to
describe the development of the intuitive faculty, personified
as Mary, Joseph merely representing the enlightened intellect.
The next higher degree of initiation is to bring the heart
quality of universal love into active expression, personified as
Jesus.   " When Herod heard these things, he was troubled."
This shows that the egoism of the lower self is afraid of being

supplanted by the inner urge to unfold more altruistic qualities. This act in the drama portrays the divergence that exists between the mystic and the materialist. It was also the portent of coming conflict between Jesus and the Jews. The fact that :

" Herod demanded of the priests and scribes where Christ should be born,"

shows that those who wielded sacerdotal power, having adopted orthodox ceremonial and the letter of the law as their career, had not evoked the Christ Presence in their synagogues, nor had they conceived the Holy Child within their own hearts. However, they knew that such a state of spiritual development could be attained in the esoteric school of Bethlehem in Judea. While Herod was in the company of the Wise Men he pretended to be interested in these spiritual matters, but he proved himself to be a cynical hypocrite. He represents the individual who is dominated by impulses from the lower self, yet envies the person who can receive the blessing of divine Light within the heart centre. He wants to retain his worldly dominion and also to secure spiritual powers ; this is not possible.

The Gospel records another quotation from the Old Testament, saying : " For thus it is written by the Prophet." However, Micah, V, 2, states :

" But thou Beth-lehem Ephratah, though thou be little among the thousands of Judah, yet out of thee shall he come forth unto Me, that is to be the ruler of Israel ; whose goings forth have been from of old, from everlasting. Therefore will he give them up, until the time that she which travaileth hath brought forth."

This was apparently written about 710 years before the birth of Jesus, and does not specifically refer to the Prophet of Nazareth. However, almost every phrase of this assumed prophecy has a spiritual significance which justifies its quotation and also calls for analysis and elucidation.

The first important feature to be noted is the supplementary name of Bethlehem, for Ephratah means : " open the way to abundant fertility and fruitfulness." Such an idea would have no rational purpose if it merely referred to a suburb of Jerusalem, but when this qualification is applied to Bethlehem as a centre of spiritual tuition, it clearly implies that within its precincts there were trained initiates of a high grade of wisdom, who also realized the Presence of God as a living fact.

The words *ruler of Israel* have a profound esoteric bearing on this theme. The title Israel was first conferred upon Jacob when he experienced an inner initiation :

> " And God said Israel shall be thy name. And the
> land which I gave to Abraham and Isaac, to thee
> will I give it, and to thy seed after thee will I give
> the land."

The word " land " suggests territory under one's control. As God is ever stimulating man's spiritual progress, we may translate " land " as a high plane of inner consciousness. It also signifies the school of mystical training and tuition which was originally established by Abraham, to preserve the divine Message he had brought to Palestine. Isaac was his spiritual son and successor, as leader of his esoteric school which was later placed under the care of Jacob, and subsequently carried on by the prophets of Israel.

This last name combines three root words of importance : " Is " comes from Isis, the Mother aspect of the Deity ; " Ra " is the Egyptian name of the divine Fatherhood, and " El " is the Hebrew word for God. So in its entirety Israel signifies the Father-Mother-God, which is the perfect ideal of Divinity. It also means " he who has prevailed with God and man." So the title : " ruler of Israel " denotes one who is the spiritual head of the schools of wisdom through which the Hebrew prophets preserved the mystery teaching that was transmitted from Abraham to David, and thence to Jesus, Bethlehem-Ephratah being acknowledged the chief centre of such tuition. Thus there was a definite but hidden purpose in the remark made by Jesus that : " Nathaniel was an Israelite indeed and without guile," for obviously he did not merely wish to say he was a Hebrew. In order to emphasize the fact that such a title and position as a ruler of Israel could only be attained as a result of an immense period of training, such as a soul acquires by repeated incarnations, Micah clearly states that the essential qualification is : " one whose goings forth have been from of old, from everlasting ! " This shows that the soul first came from the Eternal Source ; then he adds : " out of thee, Bethlehem, shall he come forth unto Me." The inference is that such an initiate can complete his spiritual development in the secret school of Bethlehem, and thereafter ascend to The Father.

The next phrase from Micah reads : " therefore will he give them up." This seems obscure until we correlate it with the propensities of the lower self, which must be re-strained during the period of spiritual training. The rest of the same sentence enforces this idea : " until the time that she which travaileth hath brought forth." This conveys a mystical significance and implies that *she* must be Psyche, the soul, who has long laboured in travail until the Christ Child be born within the heart of the initiate. So it seems clear that the objective of secret teaching given by the prophets of Israel, many centuries before the birth of Jesus, was to generate the *mystical conception* and bring to birth the Holy Child within the virginal heart of the initiate.

Reverting to the text of this Gospel, Verse 7 states :

" Herod privily called the Wise Men and enquired of them what time the star appeared."

The deeper meaning of this naïve query is that Herod

symbolizes the worldly materialist who wishes to know how and when he can develop a state of inner illumination. Apparently the Wise Men evaded a direct reply to this question. Such spiritual matters are sacred and secret, hence consistently veiled under metaphor and simile. Certainly Herod did not understand the true nature of the Christ principle, so he requested them to search with the most scrupulous care and then return and explain the essential details to him. Such a confidential dialogue is necessary in this dramatic story, because it accentuates the subsequent action with which Herod has been charged. The text continues :

" When they departed, lo, the star went before them
and stood over where the young child was."

How much useless discussion has been caused by the assumption that a star can float in the air and hover over the small space of an inn ! Is it not a metaphorical description of the inner illumination that Jesus actually manifested, and which was visible to the inner vision of his spiritual tutors ? It is the unmistakable sign of enlightenment that the Master awaits in his pupil's development in order to justify a higher degree of initiation. Similar conditions were evident in the early life of Jacob Behmen and Ramakrishna, whose teachers perceived their spiritual status before they met in person and so accepted them without delay as pupils.

It is recorded that the Magi " rejoiced with exceeding great joy." To the mystic neither time nor place exist, because these are mere aspects of the phenomenal world, whereas his consciousness is invariably attuned to higher faculties which can be used as channels for " The Spirit of Guidance."

Now the question is often asked, who were the Wise Men ? According to ancient Christian tradition their names were Melchior, Kaspar and Balthasar. Melchior is a Hebrew name which means " king of light," as Melchi means a king,

Or corresponds to Ur and indicates Light. Therefore he was regarded as a light bearer, but he also manifested the pure love quality, consequently the full significance implied by his name is : " king of light and love."

Kaspar is more recondite as to its origin and purport, and is translated as the " sacred recorder and messenger of the Gods ;" being related to Hermes it designates an " embodiment of divine wisdom."

Balthasar is still more abstruse and difficult to define. The first syllable obviously corresponds to Baal, meaning Lord, while the rest of the word signifies the spiritual wealth of human souls. In a mystical sense it implies the " Lord of power and guardian of souls."

Melchior was probably the hierophant initiator of Jesus, while his two companions acted as sponsors, they having been his earthly tutors. Thus the qualities of Love, Wisdom and Power were bestowed upon him.

Verse 11 affirms that : " They saw the young child with Mary his mother." In this spiritual drama the progressive stages of the soul's development are personified as individuals. Therefore Joseph, Mary and Jesus represent sequential characteristics of one candidate for initiation, and personify respectively the enlightened intellect, the awakened intuition and the kindled heart. The text further says : " They worshipped him." In Old English the word worship means : " worthship, that is worthiness, or possessing the quality of merit, deserving of honour and respect "; these are requisite attributes which justify high initiation.

" They presented unto him gifts of gold, frankincense and myrrh."

These are symbolic emblems, for gold represents wisdom and incense implies devotion to God with impersonal love for mankind. Myrrh, however, means bitterness, so it was presented to Jesus as a portent of his future suffering and agony of crucifixion, for it is said : "there is no Christ without the cross."

The gifts also suggest three stages of spiritual progress which he was destined to accomplish. As incense must be consumed in order to give out its fragrance, so the devotee surrenders himself in worship to God and selfless service for mankind. Gold is a symbol of the sun, and signifies the wisdom of Christ as the Messenger of God. The myrrh indicates that the final renunciation of self-hood, as implied by the cross, must precede the Ascension and attainment of At-one-ment with the Father.

> " Being warned of God in a dream that they should
> not return to Herod, the Wise Men departed into
> their own country another way."

These Wise Men were initiates of the Master grade, because they could receive direct counsel from God. The " warning " they were given is a descriptive term to demonstrate that the Herod type of individual, who seeks wordly power and holds despotic dominion over others, is not qualified to be taught the divine mysteries of inner life and the consciousness pertaining to spiritual realms.

The next verse reveals another mode of transmitting spiritual communications. The initiate, now denominated as Joseph, being of a lower grade of development than the Wise Men, could only receive a message from the Angel of the Lord, and also in a dream, saying :

> "Arise and take the young child and his mother, and
> flee into Egypt, for Herod will seek the young child
> to destroy him."

This repeated spiritual intervention in apparent human affairs indicates that the Gospel narrative does not simply refer to normal physical life, but to mystical states of consciousness within an initiate. The entire text of this story is far more sublime when interpreted in this sense. Moreover, it so plainly responds to such an elucidation that we should boldly verify which version is better. Verse 14 says :

" When he arose he took the young child and his mother by night, and departed into Egypt."

Anyone who has travelled in the Middle East will understand what a difficult and dangerous undertaking it would be for a man to take his young wife and infant child a journey of about 250 miles, the greater part of which was then desert land. It is almost incredible that such a trip could have been made without a caravan comprising assistants, and animals to carry an adequate supply of food and water. Yet traditional pictures portray Joseph as an elderly man, walking alone beside an ass upon which are seated his wife with the babe in her arms. Therefore, we are obliged to question whether this text should be interpreted literally. In like manner, if it were possible for an angel to intervene and save the infant Jesus, why should the remaining innocent children of Bethlehem not have been similarly protected ? These incongruous circumstances demonstrate that the story is not intended to deal with three persons : father, mother and child, but with three aspects of one virile young man, who " left Bethlehem by night," or rather remained *incognito* during a certain period of his esoteric training. He lived a perfectly pure life as a Nazarite, and was consecrated to the service of God. He had been trained in the mystery teachings of the Essenes, a Fraternity whose central abode was located in Heliopolis, where they preserved the wisdom of Ancient Egypt, which was sought and esteemed by great philosophers such as Pythagoras, Plato and Plutarch.

The Bethlehem centre worked under the ægis of this Brotherhood, and it is believed that the three wise men constituted the supreme council. The inference is that Jesus had reached the highest degree of initiation normally

obtainable in Bethlehem.   Therefore the three masters went
there in order to confer upon him the higher rank which
corresponds to Jesushood, this being the most exalted spiritual
status that can be given by man.   There are, however, two
senior degrees of an inner and celestial nature which can only
be bestowed from above, namely those pertaining to Christhood and The Lord.   In order to prepare for these exalted
degrees it was desirable that Jesus should go to Heliopolis
so as to complete his studies and preparation.   This period
would account for the missing years that the Gospel narratives
fail to record.

The statement that Joseph remained in Egypt until the
death of Herod is also susceptible to esoteric interpretation.
There is the danger that a young initiate may repent, or lack
courage to withstand the contrary influences of current
traditions and orthodoxy, not to mention the attractions and
seductions of mundane life, personified as Herod.   The
injunction to wait there : " until I bring thee word "
indicates the watchful eye of the Master guiding his pupil,
who must live ostensibly a normal life in the world, notwith-
standing he is passing through a most perilous part of his
journey on the Path to God.

Verse 15 contains the statement that he went to Egypt in
order to :

" fulfil that which was spoken by the Prophet, out
of Egypt have I called my son."

But this is neither the correct nor the full quotation from
Hosea, XI, 1.   According to biblical chronology his words
were written about 740 years before the birth of Jesus, and
the text should read :

' When Isreal was a child then I loved him, and
called my son out of Egypt."

On the *prima-facie* evidence this statement would refer to

Jacob before his name was changed to Israel. He was much favoured as a child by his mother, he secured his father's special blessing which should have been given to his elder brother Esau, and he actually went to Egypt to see his son Joseph ; subsequently his body was brought back to Palestine for burial. It is difficult therefore to correlate Hosea's words to the life of Jesus. It is true that some aspersions have been applied to the name " Egypt " as representing a state of darkness and tribulation, on account of the long captivity of the Hebrews there before Moses released them. As it is an acknowledged principle that a young knight must win his spurs, so a young initiate has to undergo certain tests in order to prove his merit and integrity. In this aspect it may be that the journey to Egypt meant that Jesus, or the young aspirant whom he personified, was subjected to definite trials in order to demonstrate his stability and worthiness.

The literal text of the following verse has troubled many readers, for it concerns the alleged slaughter of helpless babes of Bethlehem :

> " When Herod saw he was mocked of the Wise Men, he was exceeding wrath, and sent and slew all the children that were in Bethlehem, and in all the coasts thereof, from two years old and under."

The infamy of such a heinous crime is revolting to all Bible students, especially as it appears to have been the result of the Wise Men failing to keep an appointment with King Herod, at the *instigation of God*, in His warning to them : " to return by another way." Moreover, it was apparently the tragic concomitant to blessings they had previously bestowed upon the infant Jesus. Therefore it is necessary to verify whether this is a true historical account of an atrocity that actually happened. Apparently neither Jewish nor Roman historians have left any testimony to prove that it did actually occur. Furthermore, there arises the inevitable question, would it have been appropriate to describe such a tragic event in the nativity story of Jesus Christ? This paradoxical problem has caused many to seek a more rational alternative explanation. The esoteric analysis furnishes a perfectly logical and harmonious solution.

First, Herod is obviously a synonym indicating the egoistic power of the personality. Second, the words : " male children " signify young aspirants for Truth, and candidates for initiation who are at the stage of masculine intellect, the reasoning concrete mind. In this connection Paul said he had " milk for babes." Finally, the phrase : " two years old and under " clearly corresponds to those novices who have not yet reached the 3rd degree of initiation, and consequently they are not entitled to the rank corresponding to a full Master Mason. The inference now becomes perceptible.

In any esoteric school of mystical and spiritual training, such as the Egyptians and Essenes certainly had, there were recognised periods of probation and tuition, which were followed by corresponding tests and trials, in order to demonstrate whether the candidates were worthy and capable of advancing any further. Only " Fellows of the Craft " who gave requisite evidence of their efficiency and endurance should be raised to the rank of Master. The words that Jesus addressed to Nicodemus :

" art thou a Master of Israel and knowest not these things ? "

furnish irrefutable support to these deductions. By applying this more rational interpretation to the story it is obvious there would have been no slaughter of " the children of Bethlehem and all the coasts thereof." The deeper meaning of v 16 is that many novices of those esoteric schools were not steadfast, nor strong enough to withstand the trials and tribulations of normal mundane existence. Consequently, in a metaphorical sense, their spiritual progress was stopped, hence they were nominally *slain* and sent back to the outer world. This interpretation may convince us of the mystical truth that underlies the incredible literal text.

The next verse contains another quotation from the Old Testament, which was taken from Jeremiah, XXXI, on the assumption that it was originally written as a prophecy having a definite relationship to the alleged massacre of the Children of Bethlehem by Herod. Once again, however, it is evident that this reference is not relevant to the subject under consideration. The quotation has been wrested from its context, with an apparent intent to beguile the reader. Although Jeremiah was ostensibly giving comfort and condolence to those who were suffering, on account of the captivity in Babylon of people from Israel, about 6 centuries B.C., he also had a deeper mystical motive. Verse 18 states that :

> " In Rama there was a voice heard, lamentation and weeping and great mourning ; Rachel weeping for her children, and would not be comforted because they were not ."

Although Matthew's quotation ends here, Jeremiah continues with these illuminating words :

> " Thus saith the Lord, refrain thine voice from weeping, for thy work shall be rewarded, and they shall come again from the land of the enemy."

Apart from the possible historical reference, it is palpably clear that the author of the Matthew Gospel included this quotation in his narrative becuase it follows immediately after the descriptive acknowledgement that some novices on the spiritual Path do falter, and even recant. In an esoteric sense this implies that they are *spiritually slain* by the power of orthodoxy, materialism and mundane interests. But it should be noted that the Lord said they will recover and return to their land.

Although Rachel lived about 1700 B.C., she was regarded
as the symbolic mother of the Israelites who had been captive
" in the land of the enemy," that is, deflected from the path
by the dark forces of the Adversary. Jeremiah showed his
wise understanding of the deeper significance of this analogy,
for in his concluding verse he wrote :

> " There is hope in thine end, saith the Lord, that
> thy children shall come again to their border."

This gives assurance that despite some divergence and
delay on the journey, the true seeker after God will finally
reach His abode. So again it is apparent that the writer of the
Matthew Gospel really had a spiritual purpose by including
the Old Testament references in his narrative. It is probable
that his original manuscript contained the full quotations that
are now recorded here. It seems almost irrefutable that he
specifically sought to expound the same basic principles that
the prophets had previously given regarding spiritual evolution
and the progressive unfoldment of the human soul, by
training, tuition, and initiation into the " second birth."
This opinion supports the contention of many scholars that
the original Gospel stories were subsequently revised and
modified, in order to conform with later man-made dogmas
which were presented in substitution of the pure Christ
Doctrines given by the Master himself. To hide these
alterations and excisions it appears that the original manuscripts and early documents, pertaining to Jesus Christ's
Mission and Message, were withdrawn or destroyed.

Reverting to the quotation of Jeremiah, it is profoundly
significant that he should have so clearly stated : " a voice
was heard in Ramah," because in the careful choice of
Hebrew words Ramah is quite appropriately placed in this
statement, as it means : " the exaltation and sublimity
of a high plane." Moreover, " Samuel the prophet lived
in Ramah, and also Deborah, the prophetess lives

between Ramah and Bethel, in a hilly country of Ephraim."

Whatever may be the biographical purport of these statements, an analysis of the meanings of the words is most illuminating. Bethel means : " the house of God," and Ephraim signifies : " that which is doubly fruitful and productive." The mystical meaning of these phrases is therefore too self-evident to need emphasis, but it is obviously of far greater importance than a reference to mere localities. We may be fully assured that both the prophets and the Gospel writers were more anxious to present spiritual teaching than merely to record biographical and historical narratives of the people of Palestine. The latter have a superficial and transient interest, whereas the former make an eternal appeal and therefore justify the accredited value of a Sacred Scripture as being the inspired Word of God.

Old editions of the Bible contain a concordance and dates pertaining to the records. These enable us to verify the spiritual sequence of thought that is impregnated from Genesis to the Prophets, and which reaches its climax in the Gospels. The inner teaching of Jesus confirms that of the prophets, and emphasizes the necessity of the " second birth " in order that one might " enter the kingdom of God," which was the central theme of his Teaching. He advocated that we should follow in his steps, that is, advance by progressive stages in spiritual unfoldment, until we also can say : " not my will but Thine be done." Verses 19 and 20 continue this story thus :

> " But when Herod was dead, behold an Angel of the
> Lord appeared in a dream to Joseph in Egypt, saying,
> arise and take the young child and his mother and
> go into the land of Israel, for they are dead which
> sought the young child's life."

Once again, the perilous journey across the desert is advocated, in order to reach his native land. The esoteric

significance of this repeated intervention of the Angel is that
the young initiate requires guidance until he grows strong
enough to function consciously on higher planes and not be
inveigled by the delusions of worldly interests. To : " go
into the land of Israel " has not merely a geographical
implication, it also indicates an elevation of the directive
centre of one's activity to the more permanent state of the soul.

However, verse 22 shows that there are still dangers to be
avoided, for when Joseph :

> " heard that Archelaus did reign in Judea, he was
> afraid to go hither.   Notwithstanding, being warned
> of God in a dream he turned aside into the parts of
> Galilee."

It is important to observe that Joseph, representing the
composite initiate, must have made definite advancement in
his spiritual development, for he is now able to receive
spiritual guidance from God, instead of only from the " Angel
of the Lord " as in the earlier stages of his progress.

Assurance of the initiate's unfoldment is furnished by
emphasis on the word " Galilee ", which actually means :
" An encircled area which is filled with soul energy."   The
phrase may be interpreted as an analogy to imply raising the
consciousness to the plane of the soul, and living the silent
inner life by realizing the indwelling Presence of God.

The final verse of this chapter gives further support and
justification for this mystical interpretation.   There is a
subtle change introduced in the text, which no longer refers
to Joseph, despite the sequence of thought, but to Jesus, thus
completing the dramatic personifications previously made in
order to reveal progressive stages in the development of an
initiate.

> " And he came and dwelt in a city called Nazareth,
> that it might be fulfilled which was spoken by the
> prophets, he shall be called a Nazarene."

This last word is evidently a substitution for the more appropriate word " Nazarite," Mgr. Ronald A. Knox, in his recent translation of the New Testament, gives the following footnote : " no such prophecy has survived to us " as suggested in Verse 23. Then he adds : " Some think the word should be, not Nazarene, but Nazarite." This is confirmed by the quotation referred to in Judges, XIII, 5 to 8 :

> " Thou shalt conceive and bear a son . . . for the child shall be a Nazarite from the womb, and he shall deliver Israel out of the hand of the Philistines."

Jesus was undoubtedly a true " Nazarite," for this word means : " one who is dedicated to the service of God and mankind." It is affirmed by qualified scholars that during the lifetime of Jesus there was no such city of Nazareth in existence, though a village in Galilee has since received this name. The real significance of the word Nazareth is : " to be set apart and to live in seclusion," which his parents, Joseph and Mary had evidently done. So again, under apparent biographical disguise, there is much matter of profound spiritual import, purposely hidden in this text of Matthew. " Verily, the letter killeth, but the spirit giveth Life !"

CHAPTER VI

REDEMPTION OF MORAL DEBTS

There is a remarkable and profoundly significant story in the second chapter of Luke, wherein the author discloses how, on account of:

> " a decree from Caesar Augustus, all the world should be taxed. And all went to be taxed, every one to his own city. And Joseph also went up from Galilee, out of the city of Nazareth, into Judea, unto the city of David, which is called Bethlehem ; (because he was of the house and lineage of David ; to be taxed with Mary his espoused wife, being great with child. And so it was, that while they were there, the days were accomplished that she should be delivered. And she brought forth her first-born son, and wrapped him in swaddling clothes, and laid him in a manger ; because there was no room for them in the inn."

Luke is careful to give every detail that is requisite, but in such a manner that the text is clearly subject to a dual interpretation, that is both literal and mystical. To dwell in Nazareth means to live the inner life, while Galilee designates a higher plane of consciousness, wherein the aspirant receives the guiding influence and energy of the soul. But eventually he must descend to physical life and comply with the law : " as we sow, so must we reap."

Literally, in order that Joseph might leave those peaceful conditions and go to Judea, would necessitate a journey of over 100 miles, to be made presumably on foot. Mary would need to travel by some conveyance, or ride on an animal, which in either case would be very arduous for her.

Moreover, the question arises that if Joseph were obliged to trace back his ancestors for a thousand years, in order to pay a modest tax in " his own city " as a descendant of David, surely a similar imposition would have applied to every other man who lived in Palestine and was subject to Roman rule. The chaos and confusion which would ensue by fulfilling the letter of such a law can be imagined. In those days who would really know his own ancient lineage ? How could all the people of the country leave their homes and travel criss-cross over the land without adequate food or shelter, in order to find where their ancestors had lived several centuries previously ? The Romans are known to have established very practical principles in order to govern their empire. Why then should these irrational conditions be inaugurated ? Furthermore, even if Joseph were subject to such an impost, would he have been so imprudent as to oblige his young wife to leave the comfort of their home, and the assured attention of their near-by relatives, when she was so far advanced in her pregnancy ? These incongruous circumstances demand a more rational interpretation than can be deduced from the literal text.

From a mystical aspect, to emphasize that they sought shelter in Bethlehem, a village a few miles outside the capital of Jerusalem—" the vision of peace "—is remarkably appropriate. It is well known that Bethlehem was a centre of spiritual training during the time of the Hebrew prophets. David himself was undoubtedly taught there, and so was his father Jesse, for both received the title of " Bethlehemite."

The fact that Joseph and Mary had to find shelter in a stable " because there was no room at the inn," has been interpreted as indicating that the Master was not born of Jewry, for his parents were of the line of those ancient Hebrew teachers who were descendants of Abraham, Moses and Solomon ; but not from Judah. There were two apparently irreconcilable forms of religious teaching given in Palestine, for the prophets were inspired by the Divine Spirit and they taught mystical truth, whereas the priesthood performed sacerdotal ceremonies and expounded materialized dogmas which obscured and often destroyed the inner and spiritual doctrines, with the tragic result that Jewry rejected the Master and his teaching.

Why is such emphasis given to the unimportant episode that Joseph had to pay a tax in " the City of David ?" Is there an esoteric inference purposely veiled therein ? The deeper implication is that the aspirant on the Path to God must counterbalance his *karmic* debts before he is free to proceed on his spiritual journey of inner development. Only then can he become conscious of the kingdom of heaven within the heart, this latter being metaphorically " the manger."

The " swaddling clothes " suggests the immaturity of the young initiate, who requires careful supervision in the early stages of his unfoldment. The " inn " symbolizes the " temple not made with hands." Luke definitely indicates that Joseph " paid his tax " before the birth of Jesus occurred. Thereafter he awakened his heart by devotion to God and impersonal service to mankind. It is stated : " All went to be taxed, every one to his own city ;" this clearly implies that everybody must liquidate their past indebtedness on the *plane* whereon it was originally incurred.

> " And there were in the same country shepherds abiding in the field, . . . keeping watch over their flock by night."

This verse discloses a very delicate veil of imagery, which is employed to cover an obvious mystical meaning. Jesus later proclaimed himself to be the Good Shepherd, having other sheep not of the Palestinian fold, so we are justified in translating the text as a definite indication that the shepherds were spiritual tutors who taught in the esoteric school of Bethlehem, that is : " in the same country,"   and " by night," meaning secretly.   The following verse furnishes a subtle confirmation :

> " And lo, the angel of the Lord came upon them, and
> the glory of the Lord shone round about them,"

for only saints and initiates of a high degree become aware of the angelic presence and the glory of the Lord.

> " And the angel said unto them, fear not ; for,
> behold, I bring you tidings of great joy, which shall
> be for all people. For unto you is born this day in
> the city of David a Saviour, which is Christ the Lord."

This story is so well known and has been accepted in its literal sense for so many centuries, that there may appear to be a touch of heresy in offering a deeper interpretation. Certainly it might depict an historical episode in the life of the Master, although the reference to a " new tax " does not seem an appropriate subject to be interjected therein.

In the previous chapter Luke tells us that the angel Gabriel was sent by God to a city of Galilee, named Nazareth, to announce unto Mary the coming birth of her child.   It is therefore evident that both she and Joseph experienced supernormal states of consciousness.   It was no coincidence that they went to Bethlehem, because it was there that they received spiritual guidance and sustenance.   To " pay a tax " is a graphic allegory of a stage in spiritual evolution, and subtly portrays the beauty and essence of much mystical teaching, for " to them that hath shall be given."   It is reminiscent of the hierophant in the Greek Mysteries many centuries B.C. who urged the male neophyte to : " conceive, conceive," and then later he proclaimed : " the holy child is born."   It records another scene in the perennial story of spiritual unfoldment, which applies to all people in all ages. When the sage, saint and initiate reach this stage of advancement there is no more turning back, for their " debts are paid," their " iniquity is pardoned," their " sins are forgiven," and all errors of the past are redeemed !

Just as Mary, the intuitive faculty, " kept all these things, and pondered them in her heart," so the seeker constantly reviews in silence and secrecy the unveiling of his higher faculties.   However, the shepherds being his tutors, returned to their esoteric school in Bethlehem,

> " Glorifying and praising God for all the things they had heard and seen."

Happily, the pupil Joseph-Mary, having overcome the primary obstacles of Herod that might have impeded further progress, now voluntarily sought to adjust old karmic obligations of commission and omission.   Only thus it is possible for the :

> " heavenly host to give praise and say : Glory to God in the highest, and on earth, peace, and good will towards men,"

because this characterizes the regenerated state of the initiate.

This esoteric method of interpretation demonstrates that the doctrines of the Master constitute a sequential course of spiritual development for all who wish to experience the joyous zest of more abundant life, by accepting the hand of our Elder Brother, and co-operating with the Guiding Spirit of all humanity in the fulfilment of God's Creative Plan.

CHAPTER VII

WAS JOHN THE BAPTIST REALLY JESUS ?

The most elusive character described in the Gospels is that of John the Baptist, because his recorded life is surrounded by miracles and mysteries, from his extraordinary birth to his tragic death. The delineation of his life and conduct appears so abnormal, and lacking in the elements of conviction, that it does not reveal a truly human figure. Rather, it seems to depict a period in the spiritual life of an initiate and the progress of his soul on the Path to God-realization. It personifies the transition from an over-zealous fanatic, such as John appears to have been, to the more calm and restrained character of the illumined reformer and prophet Jesus. Thus it shows the course of progress which is requisite for an awakened soul " to see and enter the Kingdom of Heaven," and then become a Messenger of God.

Luke gives a remarkable narrative of John's origin, showing that his birth seems to have been as marvellous as the advent of Jesus. It was so circumscribed by supernatural incidents, that a mystical rather than a physical import seems obviously intended. In one single verse he introduces seven proper names, and also the Angel Gabriel, as a presage to his birth. However, these Hebrew words are profoundly significant, and they furnish much needed light on the deeper aspects to be deduced from this assumed individual.

Luke states : " In the days of Herod, King of Judea," This reflects similar conditions to those depicted at the birth of Jesus. Herod is a synonym of material and despotic force, and the inference that such power governs Judea really suggests that it has dominion over that part of human nature which should give " praise to Jehovah." This is the meaning of Judah, and it implies that the human soul is first subjugated by earthly interests.

" And there was a certain priest named Zacharias." This name means : " The Lord Jehovah has remembered, and penetrated the mind of the seeker, " who is thus imbued with spiritual ideals. The next phrase : " He ministered in the district of Abijah," infers that in the sanctuary of his enlightened mind he had realized : " My Father is the Lord Jehovah."

The text confirms this spiritual inference : " And his wife was of the daughters of Aaron." One naturally inquires why should the writer make this vague reference to a man who had lived 1,500 years previously, if not to show that she was descended from " an illumined one," which the name signifies? The next words read : " Her own name was Elizabeth." This is the Greek name that corresponds to the Hebrew " Elisheba," and it subtly designates she was : " a worshipper of God, and perceived His handiwork and blessing in human life." Further spiritual emphasis is given by affirming that :

" They were both righteous before God, walking in
all the commandments and ordinances of the Lord,
without reproach and blameless,"

To reinforce this mystical meaning, Luke states :

" And they had no child, because Elizabeth was
barren, and they were both well stricken in years."

These factors : " to be righteous, old, but childless," should be carefully observed, because they constitute necessary conditions that precede the second birth which Jesus, in his admonition to Nicodemus, said were essential before one could " see the Kingdom of Heaven." " Righteous " means just and noble conduct approved of by God ; the word " old " suggests a mature soul, one who is ready to lead the inner life

on the Path of Return ; and " childless " implies the state of a
seeker who had not yet passed through the second birth.
Luke proceeds with the illuminating remark that Zacharias
was performing his duty as a priest by " burning incense."
This is an acknowledged metaphor to express devotion to God,
because as the incense is consumed and transformed into
fragrance that rises upwards, so does the devotee eliminate all
thought of self in the elevation of his heart and in his worship
of the Lord.

The Gospel continues with these words :

> " And there appeared unto him an Angel of the
> Lord, standing on the right side of the altar of incense,"

This is another symbolic statement, for the " Angel of the
Lord " is a simile designating the human soul, which serves
and manifests the Will of the Spirit, human and divine.   The
" altar " is a synonym for the heart of the devotee, whereas
the " right side " thereof implies a positive divine injunction,
evoking a human response to spiritual guidance coming from
within.   These conjoint references show that it was an inner
experience, although it was marked by a paradox, which is
disclosed in the subsequent verses.

> " The Angel said unto him, fear not Zacharias, for
> thy prayer is heard, and thy wife Elizabeth shall
> bear thee a son. And thou shalt have joy and glad-
> ness ; and many shall rejoice at his birth."

These words reveal that the seeker, personified as Zacharias,
had long sought for inner illumination, designated as a child,
but his faith had not yet grown to an invincible conviction
that God would grant his supplication, hence his question :

> " Whereby shall I know this, for I am an old man,
> and my wife is well stricken in years ?"

The obvious contradiction between his assumed prayer for
the Inner Light, and the doubt he expressed as to the birth of

a son, is inferred with a definite purpose. This is to justify
the alleged punishment that the Angel then imposed on the
faithful old priest. Zacharias really manifests the masculine
aspect of intelligence, the objective mind, combined with
loyalty in the fulfilment of priestly duties ; but he lacked
spiritual perception.

> " And the Angel said, I am Gabriel, that stands in
> the presence of God ; and am sent to show thee these
> glad tidings. But behold, thou shalt be dumb, until
> the day that these things shall be performed, because
> thou believest not my words."

The name Gabriel implies : " the mighty man and hero of
God, a spiritual teacher and a master." In the unusual
circumstances just cited, the earnest Christian, who believes
in the unfailing justice of God, cannot but feel Gabriel's
sentence was harsh and undeserved, especially so because,
just previously, Zacharias is described as being : " righteous
before God and blameless." Alternatively, there must be a
deeper meaning underlying the text, which gives light and life
to this obscure problem. One is impressed by Luke's
definition of the son that is to be born, as it corresponds closely
to that given in Judges, XIII, 7 ;

> " For the child shall be a Nazarite to God, from
> the womb to the day of his death."

The Luke text reads :

> " He shall take neither wine or strong drink, and
> he shall be filled with the Holy Spirit, even from
> his mother's womb. And many of the children of
> Israel shall he turn to the Lord their God."

This encouraging forecast certainly promised an exceptional character. The name John, which the Angel said
should be given to the son, is an abbreviation of the Hebrew
Johanan, meaning : " Jehovah bestows grace and compassion,

and gives graciously." It should be remembered that " the dawn of spiritual consciousness" in an aspirant was referred to by the Hebrew Prophets, and also by the Hierophants of the Greek Mystery Drama, as : " a longed-for child." Such analogy gives emphasis to this story. Really it describes the process of inner development and regeneration, coupled with the gift of divine grace, which is invariably bestowed when a person " prepares the way and makes straight a highway for the Lord " within his heart.

What is to be understood by Gabriel's verdict to Zacharias :

> " Thou shalt be dumb and not able to speak until these things be performed, because thou believest not my words."

The mystic knows there are several degrees of spiritual progress, and when the centre of consciousness is being elevated above the vehicles of the lower self, it must first cross over the " bridge of enlightenment," in order to reach the higher self and the domain of the soul. During this stage of transition the aspirant can no longer freely exercise his objective intellect, because he preceives the unfoldment of a new faculty, the intuition. This is the lowest source of cognition and understanding coming from within, but it must unfold gradually before it can function fully. Therefore at one stage he is neither of this world nor of that, so metaphorically he is *dumb*, for he cannot speak with assurance from either plane of consciousness. One should not talk about this sacred unveiling of divine light within the heart, for it will eventually manifest by itself, in the life and conduct of the individual.

The fact that Luke affirms that John the Baptist was born before Jesus, and also that in each case their conception was accompanied by angelic visitations and announcements, is further proof that the Gospel records should be interpreted from a mystical, rather than from a biographical point of view.

Genesis records that Esau had to precede his more spiritually evolved brother Jacob, because they represent respectively the lower and higher self of one individual ; for a similar reason Leah was said to be older than her more advanced sister Rachel. Moreover, as it is said John was conceived six months before Jesus, it appears evident that this story was specially designed to demonstrate that the state of Jesushood cannot be unfolded or attained until the aspirant passes through the stages epitomized in the career of John the Baptist. To support this, Luke, I, 17, cites the remarkable forecast made by the Angel Gabriel regarding the promised child John : " He shall go before the Lord in the spirit of Elias."

This latter individual was an outstanding prophet of Israel who lived about 900 B.C. He championed the Cause of God with much vehemence, especially in his denunciation of Ahab, Jezebel and the prophets of Baal. Later he became more restrained and humble, as indicated in his supplication :

" O Lord, now take away my life, for I am not better than my fathers."

Now the irresistible question arises : is there a definite connection between Gabriel's prophecy that : " John shall manifest the spirit and power of Elias," and the statement made later by Jesus concerning John, as given in Matthew, XI, 14-15 :

" If ye will receive it, this is Elias, which was for to come."

Elias is another form of Elijah, which means : " my God is Jehovah." Does this not clearly imply that Jesus recognized John to be a reincarnation of Elijah ? Certainly their characteristic actions in reproving the evil of their times were similar. The further remark of Gabriel, as given by Luke : " He will turn the hearts of the fathers to the children," is worthy of analysis, because the relationship between fathers and children is also applied to the mystical bond between spiritual teachers and their pupils. The Old Testament reveals that there was continuous conflict between the sacred doctrines of the Hebrew prophets and the formal dogmas and practices of the priests, because the latter constantly sought to materialize and crystallize the spiritual teaching of the former.   This is inferred by Luke's quotation from Malachi :

' He will turn the disobedient to the wisdom of the
just, to make ready a people prepared for the Lord."

This word " Lord " represents the highest state of human consciousness ; thus Jesus first attained Christhood and finally became The Lord.   The underlying intent of these alleged prophecies pertains to all those who " hunger and thirst after righteousness."   The meaning is entirely spiritual, and applies more to inner enlightenment and development than to the physical birth of a child.

There is very little concrete information given by the Evangelists regarding the actual life of John, but the literal text of Matthew, 111, seems intended to convey a dual meaning :

" In those days came John the Baptist preaching in
the wilderness of Judea, saying repent ye, for the
Kingdom of Heaven is at hand."

In a metaphorical sense, wherever spiritual ideals and moral principles are ignored or degraded, that area becomes an arid and barren desert.   The more profound meaning of repentance is :   " a change of heart and the adoption of a new attitude to life."   This is established by those who yearn for " Light, and more Light," and who also evince a quest for divine truth, for this leads to the discovery of that condition and inner serenity which Jesus designated as :   " the Kingdom of Heaven within."

There follows a quotation from Isaiah, which is presumed to foretell the coming of the harbinger of the Lord :

> " For this is he that was spoken of by the prophet
> Esaias saying : the voice of one crying in the wilder-
> ness."

However, impartial analysis does not confirm the idea that
this was a prophecy intended to be fulfilled 700 years later in
the person of John the Baptist. Rather, it expresses the
yearning desire for spiritual unfoldment that is envisaged by
illumined souls for those who seek " peace that passeth human
understanding." Further mystical tuition is veiled in
Isaiah, XL, 1-3, which reads :

> " Comfort ye, my people, saith your God. Speak
> tenderly to Jerusalem, proclaim that her warfare is
> accomplished, that her iniquity is pardoned."

A dual inference is conveyed by the word Jerusalem, because
it is also a synonym for the soul of man, which is the inner
abode of Peace. " Warfare " is an obvious simile used to
indicate that internal conflict between the higher and lower
self, which must first be endured by the novice. When the
contest is over, and the higher self is victorious, then one's
past Karma is ended, and one's " sins are forgiven ;" in
other words, one's " iniquity is pardoned." Therefore the
phrase :

> " Prepare ye the way of the Lord, and make straight
> in the desert a highway for our God,"

is an urgent appeal expressed from the kindled heart of the
spiritual guide to the aspirant, his pupil. The " desert " is
a condition of materialism and agnostic indifference, which
however, engenders constant dissatisfaction and unhappiness
within the unenlightened individual. This apathy be must
eventually overcome and transformed by one's own volition,
in order to establish a fit " dwelling-place for the Lord," and
so acquire definite consciousness of the Divine Presence.

Isaiah confirms that this is the predestined future which must be achieved by all mankind, for he says : " Every valley shall be exalted," which implies that the humble shall be raised to a higher standard of life and spiritually elevated to a higher concept of human destiny.   " And every hill shall be made low," means that despotic, arrogant and egoistic people shall be humiliated.   " The crooked shall be made straight," suggests that the dishonest and perverse shall be reformed ; and " The rough places shall be made plane," promises that hardships in life shall be ended.

The fact that both Matthew and Mark declare John the Baptist " had a raiment of camel's hair " emphasizes that these words conceal a symbolic meaning which invites investigation and a deeper interpretation.   As the human form is really a raiment covering the soul, the inference is that the disciple must train his physical body to be like a camel, storing the essence of life's experiences, in order to endure with patient and silent goodwill the arduous toil that selfless service imposes upon a neophyte as he traverses the " wilderness " of mundane existence, ere he can reach his destination in safety.

" And he had a leathern girdle about his loins " seems an unimportant phrase, until we perceive that it demonstrates he had established a rigid demarcation between his lower and higher self.   The animal nature residing below the diaphragm must be duly restrained, and not permitted to predominate over higher attributes, whose centres are located in the heart and head.

" His meat was locusts and wild honey," are words that have caused considerable discussion, but this would have been avoided by applying the more appropriate meaning of the *locust bean*.   This is the sweet edible seed pod of the Carob tree, which is rich in protein and is a common item of sustenance in the Middle East.   In a mystical sense this dried bean is a graphic metaphor which indicates that the only spiritual food then available to the seeker after Truth was the dry and sterile residue of the Mosaic lore. Crystallized dogmas, coupled with ancient traditions and formal cere- monies, are almost meaningless to the people. However, such teaching comprised the basis of orthodoxy that was prevalent in the time of John and Jesus, and it had become so debased and materialized that it merited their denunciation.

If we accept the literal text and assume that the word " locusts " refers to insects, it seems obvious that they could not constitute food, even for ascetics. They are a terrible plague in the Middle East, therefore the implication of such an analogy is even more devastating than that of dried beans. Metaphorically, does it not suggest ravaging parasites that consume the growing crops arising from the spiritual teaching of " the Sower who went forth to sow good seed ?" Despite the efforts of people to understand the divine purpose of life and the need for a change in their mode of conduct, their idealism has been constantly destroyed before it could provide adequate sustenance for their heart and soul, and so enable them " to see, and enter, the Kingdom of Heaven."

The final reference to " wild honey " is a graphic simile suggesting that the prophet, poet and idealist invariably seek the solitude and serenity of nature as a source of joy and inspiration. There they can contemplate on the Divine Omnipresence which brings comfort to the soul and gives fuller illumination and understanding of the mysteries of life. Such was the ostensible preparation and training of the pioneer who was to : " Make straight a highway for the Lord."

Matthew's Gospel, III, 5-6, contain the curious statement :

" Then went out to him Jerusalem, and all Judea, and all the region round about Jordan, confessing their sins."

This cryptic reference to three geographical localities appears to imply that the populace flocked to meet John the

Baptist, to repent, confess their sins and to be baptized ! In a literal sense this would not only impose a colossal task for one man to accomplish, but it would also indicate that about one third of the population of Palestine were really anxious to modify their attitude to life, and also to adopt a more austere regime for their future conduct. However, history does not confirm this assumption. There is no evidence to show that John secured many loyal followers, and, to judge from the difficulties that Jesus subsequently encountered, they did not even acknowledge the Master. Hence we are faced with a dilemma, which apparently can only be solved by deeper analysis of the text.

The implied enthusiastic response of all the inhabitants of Judea would have been rather overwhelming. If John had been able to exert such a preponderate influence on the people in so short a time, there is little doubt that the sacerdotal members of Jewry would have taken drastic measures to counteract it.

The solution of this problem lies in the true significance of the Hebrew names employed. For example, as " Jerusalem " means : " the vision of peace," only those people who had already become detached from worldly standards of value and the bondage of base materialism, and also had sought spiritual serenity, would have understood John's mission. There is rarely any vision of real peace experienced by those who are still involved in the quest of excessive possessions. It is not wrong to own property, for the sense of hunger must first be gratified on the physical plane, before it can manifest fully in mental and spiritual realms. Only after such desires have been responded to can the famished soul demand its own satisfaction.

In a similar manner the name " Judah " suggests : " those who give praise to the Lord " and render thanks for their blessings of life and human faculties, rather than make supplications for something more. Again, the word " Jordan "

indicates " the river of God " and denotes : " the influx of
life that descends and flows abundantly." Therefore, to be
baptized in the Jordan is to receive the benediction of that
vital force which sublimates the entire being of the aspirant.

It is therefore evident that these three groups might mean a
very small number of people who could really respond to the
call of John. " To repent " is not merely to be sorry for some
misdeed, it also suggests : " to let go of old conceptions and
irrational traditions."

Verse 7 states that when John saw many Pharisees and
Sadducees come to be baptized, he denounced them :

> " O generation of vipers, who hath warned you to
> flee from the wrath to come ?"

Wrath suggests the *karma* or consequence of our thoughts
and deeds, for " as we sow, so must we reap," that is the law
of divine Justice.

The Pharisees were a separate and exclusive sect that
attached the utmost importance to ritual and ceremony.
They did not acknowledge the miraculous works of Jesus,
because he was not a member of their group. They demanded
proof of his Christhood, but this could not be demonstrated to
their objective intellect. The Sadducees are regarded as the
materialists and rationalists of that time. They were self-
satisfied with the reasoning of their minds, and could not
accept the evidence of the spiritual powers and faculties of
Jesus, nor did they understand the immortal nature of the
soul. Obviously such people felt little remorse for their
egoistic mode of life. They merely relied upon their
ancestry, and the assumption that they were the " elect of
God " because of their alleged descent from the Hebrew
prophets, in consequence of which they needed no redemption.
John the Baptist's remarkable statement :

> " God is able of these stones to raise up children
> unto Abraham,"

was certainly too abstruse for them to understand. But the inference is that despite the petrified and materialized dogmas to which the original Mosaic doctrines had been degraded, there was still an element of spiritual vitality in them, at least for those who understood mystical truth. His remark :

> " Now the axe is laid unto the roots of the trees,
> and every tree that bringeth not forth good fruit
> is hewn down,"

is also metaphorical. What does the axe designate, if not the new Message of spiritual teaching which was then being given, and which would cut into the foundations of the priestly practices of Jewry. Moreover, as the word *tree* is a synonym for a spiritual teacher, those who did not expound religion in a manner that would uplift the people's hearts to God, would be cut off from the Divine Source of inspiration.

Then John compared his own modest stage of spiritual development with that higher degree manifested by Jesus, in Matthew III, 2 :

> " I indeed baptize you with water ; but he that
> cometh after me is mightier than I, whose shoes I am
> not worthy to bear ; he shall baptize you with the
> Holy Spirit, and with fire."

The Spirit is the superlative faculty of man, while fire symbolizes the enlightened mind. Therefore, the little personal self, which hitherto sought everything for its own self-satisfaction, must give way to the demands of the kindled heart and illumined soul which represent the true individual, the only part of man that can reach the Kingdom of God. So it is true that : "He must increase, but I must decrease ;" because when the spiritual understanding is awakened, it constantly seeks higher illumination and the release of the soul from mundane bondage, whereas the lower self gravitates to its own level of minor importance and earthly interests.

John the Baptist represents the enlightened intellect and its logical perception of Truth, but it is not yet quickened by the Holy Spirit. However, as the herald of the Master, he could give preliminary teaching which might cleanse the heart of base hypocrisy, and the mind of false assumptions and personal egoism, these being the chief impediments to man's spiritual progress. The higher mystical form of baptism that was conferred by Jesus is the inner illumination which is subsequently reflected in the Love, Wisdom and Power of Christhood. The " wheat that is garnered " means the living grains of Truth which must be preserved by the seeker, whereas irrational credulity and meaningless formality are like useless chaff that is consumed in the living fire of Divine Light and Wisdom.

Reverting to Luke's Gospel, he demonstrates the close relationship that united John with Jesus. Immediately following his statement that Elizabeth, the wife of Zacharias, had conceived, he proceeds to describe how the Angel Gabriel was sent by God to announce unto the virgin named Mary :

> " Hail, thou that art highly favored, the Lord is
> with thee : blessed art thou among women. . . .
> Behold thou shalt conceive in thy womb, and bring
> forth a son, and shalt call his name Jesus. . . . Behold,
> thy cousin Elizabeth, she hath also conceived a son in
> her old age, . . . who was called barren."

The name Mary implies the intuitional stage in the soul's progress. The problem that now calls for solution is whether the writer of Luke's Gospel is merely narrating two concurrent biographical events that were accompanied by abnormal circumstances, or does he seek to delineate the much more profound features of the psychological and spiritual progress of the soul towards the Kingdom of God ? Just as in a Bach fugue the primary theme is constantly reiterated and elaborated, so in the Bible the awakening of higher faculties is repeatedly emphasized.

The statement in Luke, I, 26, reads :

" And in the sixth month the Angel Gabriel was sent
from God unto a city of Galilee, named Nazareth."

This contains a subtle but significant suggestion, for when
Hebrew writers employ definite numbers in an apparently
naïve setting, they invariably disclose some other profound
fact.   In the Mosaic system of numerology, number 6 is the
cypher used to indicate : " equilibrium and due fitness of
conditions that lead to a higher accomplishment," as implied
in the number seven.   Therefore it does not simply mean a
period of six months, but that a definite stage of inner development has been achieved by the aspirant.

It should also be observed that the words : " city of Galilee,
named Nazareth," are but a veil to conceal a much deeper
implication.   Galilee is a Greek word drawn from the Hebrew,
and really means : " the plane of soul energy," whereas
Nazareth indicates : " to be set apart in seclusion,"   The
inference is that the earnest seeker is under angelic guidance
from superphysical realms, and voluntarily procures a place
of solitude in order to contemplate on the Presence of God.

It is therefore evident that Luke, under cover of this disguise
and the various characters of his story, wishes to describe the
abstruse principles of spiritual advancement.   This begins at
the stage of the enlightened intellect of the neophyte, personified as John, and passes on to the intuitional faculty of Mary,
then onwards to the state of inspiration and loving service in
the person of Jesus, and finally reaches the illumination of the
Christ.   This reveals the pre-ordained destiny of all mankind,
for each one may hasten his progress by aspiration and
volutary effort.

It is worthy of note that Mary expressed to Gabriel a
similar doubt regarding the " promised child " to that
evinced by Zacharias, for Luke, I, 34, records her surprise and
question : " How shall this be, seeing I know not a man ?"

Yet the Angel's reply to her was entirely different; in fact, he pronounced a benediction instead of an alleged punishment as imposed on the priest :

> " The Holy Spirit shall come upon thee, and the power of the Most High shall overshadow thee."
>
> (Authorized version)

> " Hence what is born of thee will be called Holy, Son of God."
>
> (Moffat translation)

Other translators insert the word " the " before the phrase : " Son of God ;" but obviously this is intended to convey a very different meaning. Apart from its general import the word " Holy " implies " whole and complete." This is the correct idea in the present instance, as it indicates the full unfoldment of all latent human faculties, for in a mystical sense it is only the awakened consciousness of Christhood within an illumined soul that makes one perfected and whole. Then one is indeed holy and sanctified, and the title " Son of God" is conferred upon him from On High. Paul indicates this in saying that the Baptism of John meant the " putting on of Christ," and also that : " the Mysteries are reserved for the Perfect ones."

Before this state can be achieved there are certain psychological conditions to be transcended. When the aspirant commences to unfold spiritual attributes he cannot immediately understand the nature of these faculties, nor realize that it is possible to acquire knowledge and inner understanding without books and professors ; hence the doubt so frankly expressed by Joseph and Zacharias, who both personify the intellect. Students of mysticism will perceive that the two women, Elizabeth and Mary, are expressions of the preliminary faculties of insight and intuition, which constitute the portal to the higher self. By such analysis it is clear that the apparent unjust treatment meted out to Zacharias, in contrast with the blessing bestowed upon Mary, is simply a dramatic mode of indicating the different stages of development they each represent.

It is evident that the objective mind of Zacharias could neither understand, nor accept, the assurance that there are higher forms of learning and cognition than simple scholastic methods of study and tuition. However, the very words of our vocabulary, such as insight, perception, enlightenment, intuition, inspiration, illumination and revelation, are all derived from actual experiences that have been recorded in the lives of numerous artists, poets, painters, musicians, philosophers, saints, scientists, seers, sages and masters. This Aquarian Age has once again to proclaim and prove that man is a dual being, comprising the three dimensional personality with the physical body, emotional nature and objective intellect, and in addition the threefold individuality which includes the subjective mind, devotional heart and illumined soul.   These six composite faculties are permeated and encompassed by the seventh and highest attribute, which is the human-divine Spirit. When the consciousness is elevated to this plane the individual merges into the Universal, and thereby attains conscious " Union with The Father," as was accomplished by Jesus Christ.

If the more profound significance of these pseudo-biographical records be applied, it will be found that in spiritual evolution there is definite and sequential development of superphysical faculties slowly taking place within the aspirant.   However, the state of Jesushood was not the outcome of expanding the concrete intellect by further accumulation of earthly knowledge.   In this sense it is correct to affirm that Joseph was not the father of Jesus.   The state of consciousness described as the kindled heart, or Jesus, arises as a response to the irrepressible hunger and thirst of the soul for Truth, which is its proper sustenance. Thus it is an inner process actually stimulated by the Holy Spirit, that divine Light which resides within and beyond the human

soul, and is ever urging man to fulfil his spiritual destiny.
Luke's statement, I, 39 :

" Mary arose and went into a hill country to salute
her cousin,"

is an allusion to the attitude of prayer and mediation that
raises the consciousness of the seeker to a higher plane of
activity. It would appear from the text that Elizabeth
manifested unusual prescience when Mary visited her, by
saying :

" What have I done that the mother of my Lord
should come to me ?"

Was this a subsequent interpolation, inserted when the
Gospels were translated and revised, or is it part of the
original manuscript in which there is a metaphysical counter-
part with a deeper spiritual meaning than the words imply ?
Actually it indicates the growing power of perception in the
aspirant, when he or she reaches the stage of insight, as
characterized by Elizabeth. Then one may realize that
when the intuition, Mary, becomes mature, it leads on to the
unfoldment of a higher faculty, described as the birth of the
Holy Child, Jesus, within the devotional heart, called the cave
or manger.

These two nativity stories were both circumscribed by
supernatural events, and accompanied by angelic visitations
and prophecies. Although it is recorded that Jesus was the
son of a virgin and that John was born of an aged and barren
woman, each of these contrasting features provides the essential
conditions for the mystical second birth within the aspirant.

The inner anointing and Christhood of Jesus as a fully
illumined soul apparently took thirty years to develop
completely, because it only became manifest at the time of
his " baptism in the Jordan," The cumulative evidence of
Gospel records shows that John the Baptist was a personification of the first part of the Master's mission, preparing the

way for inititation into the Jesus life ! The entire spiritual progress of the soul and its sequential stages of development are revealed in the principal characters of the Gospel stories.

An apt question has arisen that if Baptism by water is an efficient ceremony for the remission of sins, why did Jesus himself insist on being baptized ? Surely he was not culpable, but was without sin, stain and stigma. Some explanation is given in Matthew, III, 13, which says :

" Then cometh Jesus from Galilee to Jordan, unto John, to be baptized of him,"

The deeper meaning is that the Master, having elevated his consciousness by prayer and contemplation to the realm of the soul, Galilee, then returned to the normal state of his personality, as John, so that his entire being could be illuminated with the conscious presence of the Holy Spirit. In the mystical sense it demonstrates how Jesus became immersed in the sacred stream of recreative and regenerative power, and received the divine influx of inspiration and inner guidance.

Jesus being 30 years of age indicates the long process of spiritual development which must ensue after the first initiation of the mystical rebirth of the initiate. This age of thirty is recognized as the appropriate stage in life for the coming of spiritual enlightenment, representing three times ten, that is, when the triple nature of the lower self has reached perfect development.

V. 15 adds :

" For thus it becometh us to fulfil all righteousness,"

This means " to do that which is right and acceptable by God " in the fulfilment of His Divine Plan. Baptism by water implies an inner cleansing of the personality, or the lower self, this being a prerequisite for further progress on the Path to God, and in this aspect John performed that ceremony.

The Gospel of Matthew records that when Jesus was baptized :

" Lo, the heavens were opened unto him, and he saw
the spirit of God descending upon him like a dove,
and lighting upon him,"

This demonstrates that it was an inner experience accompanied
by a celestial vision, representing an advanced initiation
conferred specially upon him, as the higher self, and elevating
his consciousness in love, wisdom and power far above the
normal status of John, personifying the lower self.   Otherwise this would appear to be the only ceremony on record
whereby the candidate is raised to a higher degree than that
of his initiator.

Another problem is encountered by assuming that John and
Jesus represent the lower and the higher self of one individual.
The mystical explanation is that the seeker, who passes through
the preliminary degrees of spiritual development, is first a
normal human being, and may well correspond to John.
Although he advances on the Path and becomes a high
initiate, such as Jesus was, he must still use a physical, albeit
regenerated form.   During his progress there is an essential
and gradual process of purification of body and mind, which
evokes a downpouring of spiritual benediction, rightly
symbolized as the descent of the Holy Spirit.   This may be
experienced as a slow but systematic process of inner refine-
ment, sublimation and attunement, together with the unfoldment of certain higher centres of consciousness, known as the
etheric chakras.   This development enables the initiate to
receive and respond to finer vibrations of an ethereal and
spiritual nature, which he is able to understand and interpret
as intuition and inspiration.   Thus he becomes definitely
conscious of celestial states of being, and he knows for a fact
that more sublime spheres of life do actually exist, although
they are beyond the range of normal human preception.

It may now be asked why did Jesus refuse to baptize other
people ?   Presumably it was because he would not impute to

them any transgression, as he fully understood human nature and realized that the conduct of each individual reveals his actual state of spiritual progress. He was always severe with himself, but full of compassion towards others. He did not even acknowledge the transmission of so-called original sin, imputed much later to Adam and Eve for their alleged disobedience. Moreover, if baptism confers upon infants and credulous people the privilege of becoming " children of God and inheritors of the Kingdom of Heaven," why did Jesus emphasize the necessity of " being born again " even to *see* the Kingdom, this state being an obvious precedent to " entering therein ?"

The rite of baptism was performed during many centuries before the time of Jesus in various countries, such as Greece, Egypt and Persia, so John was not the first to inaugurate it. Just as the Hebrew prophets had urged the people to " cleanse their hearts," so Plato affirmed : " It is the inner and not the outer purification that makes a man fit to enter the Presence of God." The earlier mystical meaning attached to baptism was to *drown the lower ego* in order that the regenerated self might arise out of the Sacred Stream. In a deeper sense it means " merging into the conscious Presence of God."

Jesus did not perform the ceremony of baptism by water, and he definitely raised the question as to its real nature in his words :

" The baptism of John, was it of men, or was it from the heavens ?"

The logical deduction is that baptism should be an inner process, wherein the candidate becomes flooded with living Light. This bestows upon him new life, an increase of power and the consciousness of higher planes of being. Such a definite downpouring of spiritual vibrations makes one polarized in all the bodies, bringing them into harmony, thus making the individual a channel to receive and transmit the

Divine Life, which is ever seeking to manifest through more perfect vehicles of expression. All World Saviours belong to this category.

There is no doubt that Baptism possesses and confers magical powers of purification, protection and benediction when rightly performed by a worthy officiant, or Master, on an earnest candidate. It is worth noting that deep significance was attached to Baptism in the ancient Mystery cults, where it was regarded as a seal, or sign, of spiritual illumination.

Jesus himself is our example, because for him the Baptism in the Jordan, or River of God, was the end of his preparation for his mission. However, first he had to endure the tests and trials of " the temptation of the devil," in the wilderness of earthly existence. Only after he had overcome the wiles of the adversary, thereby proving he was master of his three-fold personality, and immune from the seductions of pride and vainglory, could he begin his selfless labour of loving service as the Messenger of God, who sought to save mankind from the thraldom of mundane life.

Many earnest Christians have been unable to resist silent questions and searchings of heart over the imputed indifference that Jesus manifested concerning the fate of his cousin John. The writer of Matthew's Gospel dismisses the incongruous incident thus :

> " Now when Jesus heard that John was cast into prison, he departed into Galilee,"

This implied apathy of the Master seems incredible. First it should be noted that this statement follows the conclusion of his Temptation, and so establishes another significant link between the two characters. Although that graphic picture of inner conflict suffered by Jesus is described in eleven short verses, it probably reveals the synthesis of a long period of mental doubt and affliction. It reflects his anguish when he

realized that the first presentation of his Message was rejected
by the people of Palestine.

In his personification as John he was involved in bitter discussions with the leaders of Jewry, with whom his manner had
been caustic, condemnatory and without compromise, the
result being that he made enemies.   Moreover, he had reproved Herod, the Governor of Galilee, for taking his brother's
wife in marriage :

> " For John said unto him, it is not lawful for thee
> to have her."

Consequently, Herodias bore him unremitting enmity until
the end of his life.   Therefore, it seems he suspended his
public activities for a time, and Matthew's record shows that
there was a definite period of at least forty days when " Jesus
was alone in the wilderness," that is, between his baptism
and the commencement of his final mission.   This was an
occasion when he reviewed the course of previous events with
the utmost concern, though it seems his life once more had to
fit into the mystical pattern designed by the Hebrew prophets,
for it is recorded he went to Galilee :

> " That it might be fulfilled which was spoken by
> the prophet Isaiah, the people which sat in darkness
> saw a great light,"

Actually this scene of light ensuing from darkness might well
apply to Jesus himself when he perceived the possibility of
greater success if he would assuage the method of his teaching,
by making a more intense appeal to the hearts, rather than
seeking to convince the objective minds of people.

Another puzzling feature which should not be ignored is
that John and Jesus were apparently cousins, and also
Nazarite brethren imbued with similar ideals, yet there is no
record to show that they were intimate friends.   An even
closer bond of heartfelt comradeship should have been
established by the fact that John was presumably the initiator

of Jesus at his baptismal ceremony. Such a spiritual link
should have been regarded as sacred and unbreakable. Since
the entire conduct of Jesus manifested a compassionate desire
to help his countryman, would it not have been more com-
patible with his character and mission if he had tried to assist
John, either by making an appeal for his release from prison,
or at least by visiting him there and giving him some friendly
solace in his lonely captivity, as his unknown disciples
apparently did. On the contrary, as soon as Jesus knew John
was taken into custody : " he departed from that place " and
went into Galilee ! On the face of this Gospel statement such
action reflects callous indifference quite unbecoming to a saint
and sage such as Jesus ; hence our dilemma.

A solution of this paradox is provided when it is realized
that these characters were two different aspects and stages in
the development of one individual. John represents the first
tentative efforts of the zealous reformer, whose vehement
denunciation engendered reactions and animosity from the
people ; this caused him to suspend that form of teaching.
He then unfolded and attained the state of Jesushood, the
grade of initiation corresponding to the second birth, which,
he informed Nicodemus, is only possible after one reaches
manhood. It is significant that this name " Nicodemus "
means : " One who has achieved victory over the lower self ;"
moreoever, he was a private pupil of Jesus. This brought
into active consciousness and expression the faculties of his
higher self, which were more fully awakened by the benediction of the Holy Spirit at his baptism. In order to extirpate
all egocentric propensities he was obliged to endure the subtle
trials of temptation, and to surmount the enticement of occult
power, social prestige and wordly dominion for self-interest.
He thus became loving, patient and tolerant, irradiating a
comprehensive understanding of human frailties which no
longer merited condemnation but called forth his heartfelt
compassion. Therefore he adopted a more conciliatory

approach by speaking in parables to convey his moral teaching.

The meaning of " John the Baptist being cast into prison "
is that the worldly outlook of his rational intellect was surmounted and no longer permitted to dominate his conduct,
but was subordinated by his wiser understanding. Thereafter he did not resort to logical arguments and mental
discussions with the Pharisees and Sadducees, but consistently
manifested a sympathetic appeal to the populace. It was in
this manner that Jesus *imprisoned his own mind* and began to
work in Galilee, that is, from the plane of his soul. This fact
explains the anomaly of his apparent unconcern when John
was incarcerated, for it was an expression of his own development.

Some justification for this conclusion is furnished by
Matthew, for it would otherwise be strange that Jesus should
commence his final mission by uttering the same words as
John had previously employed. Matthew, IV, 17, reads :

" From that time Jesus began to preach, and to say :
Repent, for the Kingdom of Heaven is at hand."

This is the same appeal as that ascribed to John, in Ch. III, 2.!
Still more noteworthy is the record that Jesus uttered the
same extraordinary denunciation as the one accredited to John
the Baptist : " O generation of vipers," vide Matthew III, 7,
and XII, 34. Surely it was not a coincidence that Jesus
should repeat in his renewed exhortation the words and ideals
already enunciated by his forerunner and cousin, who was
subsequently imprisoned ; nor would it be an oversight on
the part of the Gospel writer to repeat them. Therefore we
may safely regard this as another well designed link, purposely
made to demonstrate that " the twain be one."

There is a more subtle allusion which seems to affirm the
identity between John the Baptist and Jesus Christ, although
it appears to reflect superficial curiosity on the part of his
disciples. Undoubledly a deeper implication lies in the

dialogue, which justifies its record. In Matthew, XVII, 10-13, we read :

> " And the disciples asked him, saying, why then say the scribes that Elias must first come ? And Jesus answered and said unto them, Elias truly shall first come, and restore all things. But I say unto you that Elias is come already, and they knew him not, but have done unto him whatsoever they listed. Likewise shall also the son of man suffer of them. Then the disciples understood that he spake of John the Baptist."

The previous verses of this chapter describe how the three disciples, Peter, James and John, had just seen a vision of Elias in the presence of the Master. This contiguity suggests they had purposely been given visual evidence of the close relationship that existed between Jesus and his previous incarnation as Elijah. Together John and Jesus certainly did restore all things, if by this is meant the mystical teachings of the Hebrew prophets. The Mosaic doctrine that is disguised in the allegorical stories and pseudo history of Genesis is very similar in style to that which is now unveiled in the Gospels. Therefore it seems most probable that Moses was an invisible guide who led Jesus up to the Transfiguration, the third great initiation. This suggestion is supported by the affirmation made by Jesus that he had come to fulfil the Law of Moses and the prophets.

As though to emphasize further the intended identity between Jesus and John, and reveal their previous and present states of being, there is the very curious question which Jesus himself spontaneously addressed to his disciples, as recorded by Mark, VIII, 27-8 :

> " Whom do men say that I am ? And they answered, John the Baptist ; but some say, Elias ! And he said unto them, but whom say ye that I am ?

And Peter answered and saith unto him, Thou art
the Christ."

Surely the logical inference is that by means of this dialogue
Jesus declared that in a past incarnation he was known as
Elijah, and in his present life he began his mission in the
character of John ; subsequently he advanced to the state of
Jesushood and finally reached the goal of Christhood, thus
showing us the Way, the Truth and the Life of spiritual
evolution.

It is affirmed that Jesus was really the " first fruits " of
our humanity, that is, he was the first of our human race to
attain prefection.   Therefore it is right to regard him as our
Elder Brother, Leader, Example and Teacher.

In the eleventh chapter of the Matthew Gospel the unknown
author gives an ingenious but illuminating exposition of
progress in spiritual unfoldment of the initiate who is seeking
God-realization.   Verse 1 states :

" When Jesus had made an end of commanding his
twelve disciples he began to preach and teach in the
cities."

In a literal sense this implies that he appointed 12 adult pupils
to be companions, whom he taught concerning the nature of
the second birth and the Kingdom of Heaven.   Apart from
Peter, James and John, there is very little recorded about the
lives and characters of the other disciples, except Judas.
But these three are so delineated as to reveal particular stages
in the development of an initiate.   Peter represents the
enlightened intellect, James the intuition and John the heart
of devotion.   It is therefore permissible to correlate the
disciples and Jesus Christ with the faculties that constitute
the completion and perfection of man, by the full development
of the five external senses of the lower self, and the seven
chakras corresponding to the etheric centres and the higher
self.   A similar inference may be deduced from King

Arthur and his twelve knights. To have control over, or to command all these faculties would justify Jesus in assuming the mission of a spiritual Teacher, because the four highest centres endow an initiate with intuition, inspiration, illumination and finally identification with The One.

> ' Now when John had heard in the prison of the works
> of Christ, he sent two of his disciples, and said unto
> him, art thou he that should come, or do we look for
> another ?"

John represents the state of the candidate who is self-conscious, but has not yet attained the cosmic consciousness of Christhood. He had developed certain spiritual qualities which enabled him to imprison, or repress, the activity of the objective mind, in order to unfold and exercise higher faculties which are referred to as the " two disciples," his subjective mind and the heart centre. These would qualify him to begin to unfold or approach the still higher attributes of the soul, which confers inner illumination, herein referred to as : " the works of Christ," Until this spiritual attribute is adequately functioning he may not correctly discern or understand its real nature, hence his anxious inquiry and the descriptive response given by the Master. It was by means of such dramatic dialogues that Jesus revealed much of his innermost teaching.

> " Jesus answered and said unto them, go and show
> John again those things which *ye do hear and see*."

First, it will be noted that Jesus is presumably addressing two men who have been, and still are, the disciples and companions of the imprisoned John the Baptist, and who have merely come to bring a message from him and receive an answer from the Master. Yet Jesus states that they " hear and see those things " that *he* is actually doing. He thus definitely indicates that they were constantly in his company and therefore must have been his own disciples. Alternatively, they and John may personify the three stages of unfoldment that precede the illumination of the soul.

> " The blind receive their sight, the lame walk, the lepers are cleansed, and the deaf hear, the dead are raised up, the the poor have the Gospel preached to them."

There is great importance in this literal record of miraculous accomplishments, because it shows that one who attains Christhood also becomes a channel for divine creative and regenerative power. But is there not a deeper mystical meaning implied in such words ?   For " the lame to walk," indicates that those seekers who had hitherto halted and hesitated had now firmly placed their feet on the Path of return.   The " lepers that are cleansed " suggests that those who were previously self-indulgent, immoral and debased had begun a course of self-discipline and reform in their lives. The " deaf who hear " implies that people who had not previously understood the orthodox Mosaic Law were then able to perceive its spiritual meaning.   " The dead are raised up " does not mean revivifying defunct corpses, because on other occasions Jesus used the word *dead* to indicate those who were spiritually asleep ; e.g., " let the dead bury their dead." Hence, the inference is that he " awakened " some people, who consequently recognized their personal responsibilities as well as the sublime beauty and spiritual purpose of life. " And the poor have the Gospel preached unto them " might be restricted to mean that he was only preaching to poor people.   But the esoteric implication of these words is far deeper, because " to be poor " was the first essential qualification for discipleship.   This word *poor* does not mean to be destitute of normal subsistence, for extremes of either poverty or wealth tend to obstruct spiritual progress, because they make the individual too self-conscious and earth-bound.   Therefore to be " poor " designates appropriate modesty and lack of egoism which enables one to become responsive and willing to receive the true sustenance of the soul, which is spiritual teaching.

" And blessed is he whosoever shall not be offended
in me."

What can the spiritual import of this affirmation be, other than to stress that when the enlightened seeker perceives a glimpse of the beatific vision through the illumination of the soul, he must not doubt its veracity, nor ignore its benediction.

Jesus is obviously speaking from the plane of Christhood, therefore he explains its nature to the initiate who may attain a similar exalted state with the primary degrees of universal consciousness. He should not be surprised when he acquires expanded vision into spiritual realms, nor disdain such revelations, because this development is the pre-ordained gift of God to man.

Now it should be noted that there immediately follows a series of penetrating questions concerning John the Baptist, and although Jesus apparently addresses them to the people, he also gives the requisite answers. This is another example of his skilful method of unveiling essential characteristics of one who is seeking the highway that leads to the " birth of Christ " within.

Verse 7 states that Jesus asked one group :

" What went ye out into the wilderness to see ? A
reed shaken with the wind ?"

First observe he refers to the *wilderness*, because it was reminiscent of his own period of trial and temptation. He also suggests the somewhat harsh conditions of mundane life, where one may work in competition with others for a bare livelihood, or merely perform dull daily duties that are like an arid desert, barren of any spiritual idealism. In such conditions there are many individuals whose interests pass quickly from one scene of activity to another. They are not one-pointed, but weak, unstable, and vascillating characters who are diverted by every passing attraction. Such people cannot make rapid progress on the journey to God-consciousness, such as John was presumably striving to accomplish.

Verse 8 is addressed to another group :

> " What went ye out to see ?   A man clothed in soft raiment ?   Behold they that wear soft clothing are in king's houses."

In other words, an easy life of comfort, vainglory and self-indulgence does not lead to Christhood. V. 9 is more precise :

> " What went ye out to see ?   A prophet ?   Yea, I say unto you, and more than a prophet."

But a prophet is a spiritual teacher who is able to commune with God and transmit divine counsel to mankind, such as Elijah, Moses and Jesus did. The context of the following verses is remarkably impressive, because it elevates the status of John the Baptist beyond that of a prophet, and Jesus introduces a paradox which is subsequently disclosed :

> " For this is he of whom it is written, behold I send my messenger before thy face, which shall prepare thy way before thee."

Here the Master clearly defines further qualifications for spiritual attainment. He first acknowledges John the Baptist was a prophet, such as the reincarnation of Elijah would naturally be. Then he adds that John was empowered to undertake a divine mission as a Messenger of God. Such a one is actually elected in the heaven-world before his human birth, and is then sent to earth with a definite Message for the world, as in the case of Abraham who inaugurated the epoch of Aries with the doctrines of monotheism. Jesus himself was actually giving tuition regarding the mystical second birth and the subsequent entry into the Kingdom of Heaven, as these doctrines were intended to be the keynote for spiritual progress during the Piscean era. So although he was nominally speaking about John the Baptist, he was really disclosing his own status and mission, and also elaborating his own teaching. Otherwise it is difficult to reconcile these statements with the assumption that John and Jesus were two different individuals. The problem becomes quite comprehensible if we understand that they personify two states of unfoldment in one character, the individual stage typifying intelligence as John the Baptist, and the universal grade of love and wisdom personified as Jesus in the state of Christhood.

In order to avoid misunderstanding the Master often repeats his mystical doctrines of spiritual evolution in another form, and so explains the progressive development of higher faculties that are bequeathed by God to man, but are still latent in most people. His exposition continues in verse 11 :

> " Verily I say unto you, among them that are born of
> women there hath not risen a greater than John the
> Baptist,"

To be " born of women " is a biological reference to persons of normal human birth, and of these John the Baptist was cited as being the most striking living example, having achieved great heights of development. It was a bold acknowledgement that no other man was greater than John the Baptist, which Jesus, in his state of Christhood, could clearly perceive. But he emphasized the unavoidable limitation of the self-conscious lower self in contrast with the cosmic consciousness achieved by those entering the Kingdom of Heaven. Therefore he added :

> " Notwithstanding, he that is least in the Kingdom
> of Heaven is greater than he."

This statement is paradoxical if applied to his alleged cousin, because John could not be even a prophet, still less a messenger

of God, if he had not already seen, and also entered the Kingdom of Heaven. Therefore it seems undeniable that Jesus
is subtly describing his own advanced states of spiritual
development, for he had become both a prophet and a
divinely inspired messenger. The Master thus defines the
degrees of development that separate the three dimensional
lower self from the spiritual perception that is acquired by
virtue of being born again. This latter state elevates the
consciousness, first into the higher self through the portal of
intuition, and then, to be able to " see the kingdom," it must
rise to the mystic heart, the plane of inspiration. This is
subsequently followed by " entering the Kingdom," which
means to unveil the illuminating light belonging to the soul,
and leads on to Christhood by the benediction or descent of
the Holy Spirit.

This differentiation of the planes of consciousness was
partially acknowledged in the words ascribed to John the
Baptist, when he said he was unworthy to unloose the latchet
of the Master's sandals. Metaphorically, he meant that
worldly knowledge could not even approach, still less understand, the mystical wisdom of Christ consciousness pertaining
to the soul.

By virtue of his own spiritual attainments Jesus was able to
distinguish every stage and to give such convincing explanations of the unfolding grades of higher consciousness predestined for man. This is the fundamental feature of his
mystical teaching, and reveals the priceless value of his
personal training which made his disciples God-intoxicated
men, and his subsequent followers such fearless martyrs for
spiritual principles.

There is no doubt that Jesus employed the term *Kingdom
of Heaven* as a synonym having a similar meaning to the word
Samadhi used by Yogis to describe the transcendental bliss
they experience. It also corresponds to the first grade of
Nirvana, as employed by Buddhists to imply the blotting out

of the limited self-consciousness of the personality, in order to surmount it and reach spiritual realms of Cosmic consciousness. This same idea is expressed by Christian mystics as *Illumination*, which must precede individual Union with the Universal Being of the Father.

There is as vast a difference between these exalted states of ecstasy and the normal three dimensional consciousness of ordinary man, as there is between this latter group and the simple consciousness of the animal kingdom. Herein lies the immense importance of the mystical doctrines expounded by Jesus Christ in his state of At-one-ment with God.

In a subsequent verse of this chapter the Master further explains the source and nature of the celestial consciousness belonging to Christhood :

> " All things are delivered unto me of my Father ;
> and no man knoweth the son but the Father, neither
> knoweth any man the Father save the Son, and he to
> whom the son will reveal Him,"

The first phrase : " all things are delivered unto me of my Father," indicates that when an initiate enters the Kingdom of Heaven he actually becomes an illuminated soul, and God " reveals all things unto him." No ordinary man of the world can realize the spiritual status of such individuals, although the sacred relationship between Father and son may be experienced by spiritual teachers and their pupils. Only God-realized souls, masters, hierophants and those who have accomplished liberation from earthly bondage, are qualified to sponsor candidates for these higher initiations, and so guide seekers further on the Path of Return. Hence the sublime benediction implied in the Master's words :

> " Come unto me all ye that labour and are heavy
> laden, and I will give you rest."

Such was the inner illumination and divine benediction that

gave him authority to teach, heal and initiate his disciples into the mysteries of the Kingdom of Heaven.

Drawn to him by an inexplicable but irresistible force, yearning souls have found in Jesus the spiritual sustenance that satisfies their hunger. Many of his followers have been encouraged to seek still higher fonts of Grace and Glory, with the earnest aspiration : " Is it Thee, my Beloved Lord ?" " No, still further am I," is the reply, until we also can proclaim : " The Father and I are one."

Now Mark, VI, 21-29, describes in graphic language the final and tragic scene in the story of John the Baptist. Its setting is the birthday feast given by Herod. However, it should be observed, not only was it " given in Galilee," the soul plane, but it followed immediately after " the name and fame of Jesus was spread abroad," thus reaffirming the close identity existing between these two characters, and showing that as " one increases the other decreases," and disappears !

> " When Herod heard of the works of Jesus he said :
> it is John, whom I beheaded, and he is risen from
> the dead."

The mystical inference is that John, representing the lower self, is now " dead," whereas Jesus, the higher self, is a spiritually " living " soul, manifesting the powers of Christhood.

The daughter of Herodias, his brother Philip's wife, had danced before the assembled guests and so pleased the king and them that sat with him, that :

> ' Herod sware unto her, whatsoever thou shalt ask
> me, I will give it thee, unto the half of my kingdom.
> And she went forth and said unto her mother, what
> shall I ask ? And she said, the head of John the
> Baptist. And immediately the king sent an
> executioner, and commanded the head to be brought,
> and he went and beheaded him in prison. And he

> brought his head in a charger, and gave it to the
> damsel, who gave it to her mother. And his
> disciples came and took up the corpse and laid it in a
> tomb."

Such is the melodramatic record of the demise of him who
was " the harbinger of the Lord," Is this true history, or is
it an allegory designed to convey some deeper meaning ?

It will have been observed from the foregoing analysis that
the entire tenor of the recorded life of John the Baptist
justifies the conviction that it is not a simple biography.
Rather, it comprises a series of inner experiences in the life
of an advocate for spiritual Truth, or one who dedicates his
life to teach his fellow men and expounds the way to the
Kingdom of Heaven.

An esoteric interpretation of the final scene of this mystical
drama confirms such a conclusion. Herod is an embodiment
of worldly power, personal will and egocentric consciousness.
He typifies the dark forces that constantly obstruct new
enlightenment and spiritual progress. He also represents the
individual who does what he likes, in utter disregard of current
laws and social customs. Herodias and her daughter are
introduced in order to present the licentious side of his
conduct, which the Master strongly reproved.

The words of Mark, VI, 23, are a concise statement having a
dual meaning : " Whatsoever thou shalt ask of me, I will give
it thee, unto the half of my kingdom." First, this reveals to
what extent such a depraved individual is caught in the coils
of his own vice. The second aspect is implied in the words :
" the half of my kindgom ;" for this obviously does not refer
to his regal estate, but rather to the lower part of his being,
his physical body and emotional nature, together with his
objective mind, all of which were prostituted by his self-
indulgence. He first surrendered himself to the seductions of
Herodias, and then to her daughter, although both may be

used as metaphors in order to accentuate the conditions of his life. Certainly, such characters would not respond to any exhortation to " repent and seek the Kingdom of Heaven," Therefore, he and his intimates openly rejected and reviled this teaching as given by John, who was thus metaphorically *murdered*. Hence the pathetic lament of Jesus :

> " O Jerusalem, if thou hadst known the things which belong unto thee ; but now they are hid from thine eyes !"

Matthew, XIV, 13, states :

> " When Jesus heard that John the Baptist had been beheaded, he departed thence by ship into a desert place apart."

This really implies that Jesus, having first controlled his lower mind, had eventually subjugated his entire lower self and personality. He then began to work from higher centres of consciousness, " a desert place apart," therefore this does not mean that he was indifferent to the martyrdom of John, or that he feared the authorities might impose a similar penalty upon him.

The verses that immediately follow are remarkably illuminating, for they describe how : " Jesus was moved with compassion towards the people." He healed their sick and proceeded to feed five thousand men, besides women and children, with five loaves and two fishes ! Thus in his Christhood he presented a more sympathetic and appealing form of teaching, giving love and true spiritual sustenance.

Thereafter he expounded the Christ doctrines of Love, Wisdom and Power, with the assurance of divine grace which superseded the Mosaic Law, surpassed the message of his erstwhile precursor, and made him the idol of the people. Thus he transformed his disciples into valiant apostles, healed those who were morally sick, and cured the sight of people whose spiritual vision was obscured. Further, he opened the minds of those who could not understand divine Truth, and entered the hearts of the sad and lonely by his all-embracing optimism and transcendent wisdom.

The difference between Jesus and John was not one of nature, but one of degree in potency, profundity and penetration. In this description of his own unfoldment we are shown how we also may stimulate our spiritual evolution and so become receptive vessels of divine Love, Life and Light, and thereby assist in establishing on earth the brotherhood of man in the Fatherhood of God.

CHAPTER VIII

THE TEMPTATION

The portrayal of the Temptation of Jesus contains many episodes which have caused questioning of mind and searching of heart, because literally they appear incomprehensible. John does not refer to the story at all, Mark disposes of it in a single verse, and brings wild beasts on to the scene, while the Luke version seems a palpable paraphrase of the narrative given in the first Gospel, which is the most sequential and mystical of all the accounts.

The temptation of the Master is recorded in Matthew immediately after the Baptism ceremony on the river Jordan, when Jesus became spiritually clairvoyant, clairaudient and conscious of the Christ Presence. The Holy Spirit then bestowed upon him a vitalizing effulgence that covered and permeated his entire being and simultaneously opened his inner consciousness to superphysical realms.

It is especially important to note that the Gospel narratives establish an unequivocal identity between the " Spirit of God descending like a dove " at the Baptism, and the " Spirit that led him into the wilderness to be tempted of the devil."

Matthew, IV, 1, leaves no doubt on this point, for it reads :

" Then was Jesus led up of the Spirit into the wilderness to be tempted of the devil."

Mark declares:

" And immediately the Spirit driveth him into the wilderness," whereas Luke states :

> " And Jesus, being full of the Holy Ghost returned
> from the Jordan, and was led by the Spirit into the
> wilderness."

A recognition that it was the Divine Spirit that prompted
his temptation, through the medium of Satan, has surprised
and shocked many earnest Christians, for it contravenes the
Lord's Prayer : " Lead us not into temptation !" Who
then is responsible if one *falls* ? Moreover, as the assumed
dialogue between these two characters was so abnormal and
there was no other human being present, it seems incon-
testable that only Jesus could have recorded it, either in
writing or by detailed description to his most intimate
disciples. These facts accentuate the spiritual purport of
this dramatic story.

The Matthew Gospel has been described as "the most
important book ever written," and its conspicuous quality
is that it contains esoteric and spiritual teaching, veiled under
allegory and symbol, which is so profound and true that only
an advanced gnostic and high initiate could have compiled it
in such unmistakably mystical language.

As an occult epic the Temptation of Jesus stands unique in
sacred literature and reveals the seal of a master's hand.
However, it would be incorrect to assume that it was recorded
merely to eulogize the Master's triumph in the tests and trials
of his character and moral principles. Although it is presented
as a dramatic dialogue, it must have occurred in superphysical
planes of consciousness, hence Jesus was the only participant.
He was obliged to encounter the accumulated stains and
stigmas of the past, to " face the dweller on the threshold "
alone, and to annul every vestige of the lower self, in order to
function as a liberated soul and Messenger of God. Before
any aspirant can develop, consolidate and exercise spiritual
attributes, he must first master his body and emotional

nature, then repel the desire for occult powers and psychic phenomena, and finally surmount all personal ambition. Therefore this narrative was designed and presented, like other inner experiences ascribed to Jesus, for the benefit and guidance of all those who desire to follow in his steps and accept him as their spiritual counsellor and guide.

In this analysis our first inevitable conclusion is that Satan is not synonymous with the human wickedness and evil doing of decadent persons whose actions are generally described as : " the work of the devil." They are invariably unevolved individuals who commit unlawful deeds, cheat the widow and orphan, rob the rich, delude the poor and even resort to murder, in order to achieve their malevolent purposes. Such people have a pathetic and tragic process of evolution and purification still to work through.

The character of Satan as described in the Gospels seems to correspond to the Adversary and Tester, who tries and proves the endurance and moral qualities of those who are travelling on the Path to God. As strength in any form is developed by overcoming an equal resisting force, this Adversary seems to be actively engaged in the service of God for the welfare of mankind. This Temptation of Jesus is reminiscent of the trials to which Job was subjected, also through the medium of Satan and with the consent of God, although that story is more allegorical than historical.

The phrasing of the three acts in this scene of the Temptation of Jesus is remarkable, but undoubtedly symbolical. Certainly it cannot pertain solely to the material plane, judging from Luke's statement :

> " And the devil, taking him up into a high mountain, showed unto him all the kingdoms of the world in a moment of time."

With this superphysical allusion we may be better able to understand its deeper significance. It is a recognized fact that at whatever stage in spiritual progress an aspirant has reached, immediately after he receives a special blessing or initiation he is subjected to definite tests, in order to prove whether he has adequately learned his lessons, and also incorporated their teaching into his character and very being. Otherwise he cannot proceed further on his pilgrimage, because he must first attain mastery over every phase and feature of his training and inner development. This must begin with his threefold personality, and in the course of his normal human and physical life in the world.

Matthew, IV, 2, appears to describe a definite period of asceticism :

> " And when he had fasted forty days and forty nights,
> he was afterwards an hungred."

The usual assumption is that Jesus literally went without food for approximately six weeks. The Luke text seems to have been revised in order to present this as a physical fact, although it does not coincide with the metaphysical features of the story : " In those days he did eat nothing." Is there not a far more subtle and profound inference to be deduced from the Matthew text ? While he was being baptized in the Jordan, immersed in Divine Light and permeated by the Spirit of the Celestial Christ, his soul was filled with spiritual sustenance and he experienced that blissful ecstasy which leaves nothing more to be desired. The dramatic contrast of being led " into the wilderness " after such a benediction is a mystical analogy, given in order to show that a human being may be, for some precious moments, elevated :

> " into the third heaven, when he sees God as
> through a glass darkly."

However, the price to be paid for such a privilege is an imperative imposition, for the individual must return to earth and carry this newly acquired celestial light down into the planes of human existence, so graphically depicted as " a wilderness." In this mundane environment there is a pathetic lack of that mystical food which the heart and soul so anxiously seek in order to satisfy their internal hunger. Instead of gratifying his own innate and insistent desires, the initiate must be ready to impart what he has already received and give to others who are still more spiritually famished. Moreover, it is true that no knowledge is really ours until we can express it in our own language.

The reference to forty days and nights has no relation to time, rather it implies four times ten, forty being an obscure and symbolic word cited in several books of the Old Testament. It suggests four realms of human consciousness, and as the number 10 is a cypher that designates aggregation and mastery on any one plane of activity, the inference is that he had completed the development of his personality. It is said Jesus was " an hungred," because one cannot find spiritual food on any of the four lower spheres, for even the intuition comes as the dawning of a new day, the first glimmering ray of Divine Light that is irradiated through higher planes, from the soul and spirit.

In this scene Jesus represents the aspirant to whom a brief glimpse of the Beatific Vision has been unveiled. Such bliss is quite literally given by the Grace of God, it cannot be commanded nor acquired at will by any individual until he has advanced much further on the journey and dwells constantly in the Divine Presence.

This temptation story is a picture of earthly illusions, subtly veiled and presented in the most enticing and persuasive form. Note the invitation :

" If thou be the son of God, command these stones
to be made bread."

How seductive it is to the natural human desire to exhibit occult powers and enjoy self-satisfaction of egoistic pride. The word " stones " was previously used as a metaphor to represent religious dogmas that had become petrified, dry and sterile. For John said :

" Of these stones God is able to raise up children unto Arbaham,"

thus indicating that there is still a modicum of spiritual truth left in the Mosaic lore, which a prophet such as Jesus could reveal.

Would it not have been much easier for him merely to have given a deeper and more mystical explanation of the teaching of Moses and the Hebrew prophets, than was then taught in the synagogues ? But it is not the mission of a Messenger of God simply to resuscitate the doctrines of his predecessors. His work is to expound Divine Truth in another guise and with a different appeal to the mind and heart. It is not Truth that alters, but the progress of civilization and human understanding that changes with each epoch ; consequently it was necessary to propound a new means of finding the Kingdom of Heaven.

Abraham and Moses gave the monotheistic axiom, there is only one God, albeit He was described as being somewhat restricted and tribal, though Majestic in Power. Solomon taught another aspect, by declaring that :

" The beauty of Divine Wisdom is far more precious than riches. Get wisdom and understanding, forsake her not, and She shall preserve thee, for the Lord giveth Wisdom, and She shall protect thee."

Jesus did not repeat these doctrines, but he fulfilled them mystically in his own character and conduct. Although his esoteric teaching was that man must be born again and enter the Kingdom, he emphasized that God is Love, thus indicating the most sublime of Divine attributes. The first of the Christ Doctrines is that we should love God with our heart and soul, in gratitude for the gift of life. How many have yet learned to apply his second axiom, " to love our neighbours as our-

selves " and so establish World Brotherhood ? So few of us
realize how very much we love ourselves and how little we
actually give to others. Jesus averred that the precepts of
power and wisdom alone are not adequate for the highest
development of human civilization. He had to encounter
and triumph over this test of personal power, when :

> " The devil taketh him up into the holy city, and
> setteth him on a pinnacle of the temple."

In a literal sense this would obviously have been impossible.
But there appears to be a veiled and adroit suggestion that, by
virtue of this spiritual wisdom and miraculous healing power,
it would have been quite possible for him to be appointed the
Chief Priest and Leader of the Sanhedrin. But then he would
have been obliged to maintain Rabbinical teaching with the
orthodoxy of Jewry, and also undertake not to create palpable
conflicts against their established customs. For the text
reads :

> " If thou be the son of God, cast thyself down, for He
> shall give his angels charge concerning thee. They
> shall bear thee up, lest thou dash thy foot against
> a stone."

How subtly veiled is the inner meaning. It is clear that
although he had attained the state of Christ-consciousness, he
was still in human form, so he might quite well " cast himself
down " in order to occupy the highest Office in the Synagogue.
Then, if he should discover some of the petrified mosaic
teaching to be like " stones " that hurt his foot, or rather
understanding, and find them incompatible with his own
spiritual illumination, surely the Angels of the Lord would
promptly help him out of his difficulties ! This was indeed
a great temptation to a zealous reformer, such as Jesus was
at the beginning of his ministry, but happily he conquered the
inveigling enticements of the lower self seeking position, power
and prestige. The Angel of the Lord is a synonym for the

soul, which is also the temple of God, the abode of Christ and the Kingdom of Heaven. These spiritual attributes cannot exonerate the egoistic self from error, nor counteract personal caprice ; such defects must be adjusted on the physical plane. The reply ascribed to Jesus : " Thou shalt not tempt the Lord thy God," seems to imply that he acknowledged that he himself was " the Lord thy God," whereas it was stated just previously that : " The Spirit of God led him into the wilderness," and the devil had affirmed : " He shall give His Angels charge concerning thee." There is an undoubted sense of duality purposely conveyed in these statements, which annuls the assumed claim of Jesus being the " Lord thy God."

Then followed the most tempting offer that could possibly be made to a man who had acquired mastery over his lower self, attained mental enlightenment and spiritual illumination, as well as the realization of his innate divinity. What is there of a mundane character that such a man could not accomplish ? All the wealth and dominion of the earth become subservient to his power. Now we see how profound were his words : " I have overcome the world." However, the decisive test had still to be endured, so :

> " The devil taketh him up into an exceeding high mountain, and showeth him all the kingdoms of the world, and the glory of them ; and saith unto him, all these things will I give thee, if thou wilt fall down and worship me."

This is similar to the bargain made with Faust by Mephistopheles, who offered him youth and wealth in exchange for his soul.

A natural question arises : what does the devil represent in being able to offer supremacy in all the domains of earthly life ? Perhaps only the power that is secured by selfish ambition, unscrupulous avarice, or political deceit and abuse. All such actions Jesus scorned with righteous indignation, as

conveyed in his laconic reply : " Get thee hence, Satan."
Such was his supreme temptation ; was he truly dedicated to
the service of God, or was he still subject to the wiles of the
world, the flesh and the devil, for his own personal pride and
self-glory ?

At some earlier stage on the Path of spiritual progress it
may be permissible for an aspirant to hold high Office, in
order to help his people and country.   However, there is
always the danger that he may become subject to the principles
or projects of the party that places him in power ; then he is
no longer free to serve God impersonally, or man impartially.
A Messenger of God must fulfil the behest of Him Who is the
One Master, and he must also selflessly serve all mankind,
irrespective of race, creed or colour.

> " Thou shalt worship the Lord thy God, and Him
> only shalt thou serve."

Having been victorious in this final test as a human being,
he was still " an hungred " for spiritual sustenance.   So
" Angels came and ministered unto him," meaning that his
Master, The Celestial Christ, continued to teach and train
him.   Thus he could say :

> " What shall it profit a man if he gain the whole
> world, and lose his own soul ?"

With this attitude it is both possible and true that a man does
receive spiritual help and the guidance of superphysical
beings.   The recurrence of this word " angels " in the
Scriptures has been interpreted as pertaining solely to past
ages, and as meaning ministers of God belonging to the devic
host.   Many transcendental beings who appear in vision
today, and who assist individuals at critical periods of their
spiritual progress, are advanced human souls who have passed
beyond the terrestrial plane of action.   In special cases they
may be Masters, members of the White Brotherhood, or

Knights of the Holy Grail, who act as our guardians and are ever ready to aid us in our need.

In this case of Jesus it was the Christ Himself, that is " He Who is the Teacher of Angels and mankind," who ministered unto him. All such beings are real and living ; although they dwell in ethereal realms they exercise conscious and intelligent activity on behalf of humanity in the service of God.

This is one of the most important facts that the present generation should recognize. It is true that " when the cry of the disciple reaches a certain pitch, the Master is there to aid him," wherever and whenever it may be. It is their presence, power, wisdom and love that enable the aspirant, or candidate for higher initiation, to prepare himself and pass successfully through the necessary tests and trials. In this manner they help to fulfil the divine Plan of Creation, which is thereby hastened forward. The more advanced the soul is, the greater his desire and capacity to co-operate with God in the service of mankind.

In such a manner Jesus was enabled to accomplish the heavy, though self-imposed labour of love, by transmitting the new Message of the Age to an incredulous and unsympathetic world. The pioneer of spiritual ideals invariably encounters criticism and condemnation, because he is obliged to present new aspects of Truth, to reveal the divine Purpose of Creation, and to reaffirm the pre-ordained destiny to be achieved by man. This necessitates spiritual evolution which can be expedited by individual effort and esoteric training, together with self-discipline, self-effacement and self-sacrifice. These principles appear to be in conflict with current orthodoxy and the conservative interests that seek to perpetuate crystallized creeds.

The assumption that the truth once given is unalterable, and must ever remain unchanged, is alien to the spirit of progress and civilization. The tragic feature of the present era is that the sacred doctrines given to the world by Jesus Christ were modified almost immediately after he left the earth plane, and materialized dogmas were substituted for them. It is therefore desirable to reaffirm the inner Teaching that he gave, for it is truly rational as well as spiritual, and is of permanent application to all phases and stages of human advancement.

The ethics he expounded in the Beatitudes will assuage the hardness of personal pride and egoism. Every individual must face such a period of temptation as herein described, in order to prove he has risen above all selfish interests and willingly renders homage to God and loving service to his neighbour. In this lies our salvation.

CHAPTER IX

TRANSFIGURATION

Of the greater initiations and inner experiences recorded in the life of Jesus, that which is called the Transfiguration is described in such obscure language that its inner meaning has been little understood. Certain mystics and initiates of modern times have regarded it as symbolizing the third major step in the process of spiritual unfoldment.

The story inscribed in the Gospel of Mark, IX, 2-10, gives the impression that the phenomenon was sufficiently manifest to be seen by the three disciples who then accompanied the Master. Yet there were evidently still deeper aspects beyond the compass of their vision, and which were revealed only to Jesus. In its literal presentation the narrative does not convince one as having occurred on the exterior plane of physical reality ; but its inner and spiritual significance is far more impressive and illuminating. An analysis of the characters of the three most intimate friends who witnessed this, and other important events in the life of the Nazarene, shows that they were real human figures ; but they also personified different psychological aspects belonging to an initiate. Their particular qualities supplement the status of Jesus himself, and thus make up a composite character which exhibits the multiple stages of unfoldment experienced by every soul on the Path to God-realization.

Although in the opening verse Mark introduces what appears to be a different subject, it is undoubtedly intended to be included as an essential feature of the superphysical experience he subsequently describes. The first problem is to solve the true meaning of the Kingdom of Heaven and to discover its relation to the Transfiguration itself. Verse 1 reads:

" There be some that stand here who shall not taste of death until they have seen the Kingdom of God."

Students of mysticism recognize that in his basic teaching Jesus sought to implant in the consciousness of his followers the ability to see and also enter the Kingdom of Heaven, not as a far distant or after death event, but as that which should be understood and realized during earthly life, and as an essential step before one can pass on to higher states of being. As it is almost impossible to define such spiritual experiences in everyday language, the great religious teachers presented their lofty idealism under the guise of simile and allegory. Hence the sublimity of the Christ Doctrines is skilfully covered by veils of imagery, which must be gently drawn aside by the enlightened mind in order to find the jewels of truth hidden therein.   The Kingdom must surely be that plane of consciousness wherein the saint, seer and sage can first observe, and then become directly aware of, the Divine Presence as a Living Reality. When this realm has been reached, one's entire life becomes transformed and attuned to the inner realization that the Deity pre-ordained a definite objective which man must fulfil by his own voluntary effort ; this is the ultimate purpose of the gift of human free will. It is obvious that Jesus perceived his closest followers could attain this ideal during their contemporary lifetime ; more- over, they recognized that the vision of the Transfiguration was a requisite step towards this achievement. Being the pioneer in this spiritual adventure, the Master was the one best qualified to present and explain this feature of the soul's pilgrimage. He left the Gospel record for our guidance and spiritual upliftment, if we will but emulate his example.

The superlative value of his teaching is that every phase of his inner experiences constitutes a sign-post to guide us on the journey to At-one-ment with the Father ; this gives us the assurance that he is our Saviour. The second verse begins with the curious phrase, " And after six days," which appears to have little meaning or purpose. Similar words precede the stories of the " Marriage in Cana," the " Feast of the Passover," and the " Raising of Lazarus," which are also apparently historical episodes, although they actually describe in a mystical sense spiritual incidents of profound importance. In the Hebrew system of numerology number six means " due fitness and proportionate measure," the appropriate conditions that will subsequently lead to higher accomplishments. Therefore, in the course of spiritual advancement the Transfiguration of an individual is a stage beyond both the Baptism and Temptation, but one that must precede the higher degree disguised as the Marriage in Cana. This latter completes the unfoldment of potential human faculties, which Jesus so effectively exercised in his ministry.

The descriptive text affirms that :

" Jesus taketh with him, Peter, James and John,
and leadeth them up into a high mountain apart, by
themselves."

This suggests that, before one can experience the Transfiguration, it is essential first to elevate the consciousness from the objective mind of worldly interests, then pass through the plane of abstract principles, as perceived by the intuition, and so reach and remain quiescent in the heart centre. In every instance where it is recorded that Jesus went up into a mountain, the deeper inference is that, by the graduated process of concentration, meditation and contemplation, he raised his consciousness to celestial planes wherein he became aware of, and immersed in the Light of the Divine Presence. This we also should strive to do, and expecially when we are faced with difficulties that appear beyond our individual powers to surmount.

In order to understand the mystical implication of the next verse in the text : " and he was transfigured before them," it should be recognized that there are several minor grades of progress in every major initiation. The Gospel record describes only the final stage of this degree, which portrays how Jesus became one of those " who are arrayed in white robes."

In the earlier stages of this initiation the neophyte is admitted into an inner Temple and presented to the Master of the Lodge who examines him with penetrating vision in order to be assured of his worthiness. The Brethren present can perceive his actual spiritual status, and so can express their approval of his admission. He is then accepted on probation and informed that his conduct in the world will forthwith be subject to the Master's supervision. Later, when he is sufficiently qualified by the development of his character and understanding, he is again taken into the Temple, and he stands before the Master, who approves of his progress. Once more he must return to his worldly career and now strive to establish justice, equity and co-operative good-will, as far as lies in his power.

After enduring many trials and tests to prove his initiative, courage and integrity, he is readmitted into the Temple, and is then impregnated with spiritual magnetism that slowly but surely permeates his entire being, and engenders the reactionary effect of kindling the latent light in his own soul. This radiance gradually increases and expands until it entirely suffuses all his lower vehicles, which inner process may take many months or even years, according to the zeal and self-effacement manifested in his conduct and outer life.

When this work is accomplished his being will be transmuted and imbued with spiritual light, whose radiance is the index of his qualification for the final degree of this initiation. In the corresponding temple ceremony he discovers that he has become gradually transformed and has grown into a radiant being, by virtue of his purity and nobility in thought and deed. The effulgent light in his soul now irradiates his whole being, making his various superphysical bodies translucent, which cover him as though with a robe of Living Light. It is this exalted state that is so graphically and briefly described in the next verse of the text :

" And his raiment became shining, exceeding white
as snow, such as no fuller on earth can white them."

In similar circumstances, when Moses raised his consciousness to heavenly spheres, his face became so radiant that his friends could not look upon him ; for " the fashion of his countenance was altered."

Henceforth it is the privilege of the initiate to be able to call upon The Father, as did the Prophets before him. Thus he becomes a witness of God and a ray of Divine Light on earth, carrying illumination wherever he goes and giving it whenever it is needed. The accompanying benediction that Jesus received is conveyed in the announcement : " This is my beloved son, in whom I am well pleased." This does not reflect a single or unique bond that exists only between him and The Father, rather, it is open for everyone to seek and attain this boon, and to know the joy of such spiritual relationship.

At this stage the initiate recognizes that his real being is an immortal soul filled with The Father's Light. He also discovers that when he originally became a living self-conscious individual, in the far distant past, the " King's Signet " was imprinted on his soul, and therein lies the mystery that abides between God and himself, the secret of his future destiny. As no two leaves on a tree are exactly the same, no two pebbles on the seashore are quite alike, so there are no two souls who can fill the same rôle in the Creative Drama. Each one is like a note in the Divine Symphony which would not be complete without the full contribution of every individual.

The crowning feature of the Transfiguration is when the divine secret of the initiate's destiny is unveiled and he is given a glimpse of the glorious future that awaits him. It will be remembered that it was after this inner illumination that Jesus foretold his betrayal and Passion, which was to be followed by his Resurrection and Ascension to the Father. Thus we may realize that we also are indispensable, and that God requires our full co-operation as much as we need His blessing of Light and Love. So we may enter into sacred union with Him as His junior partners, and offer our loyal service until His Will shall be fulfilled.

The Gospel contains only an abbreviated record of this final scene, because Jesus had already passed through the minor degrees of this initiation, and only needed to recapitulate and synthesize the essence of these inner experiences, in order to bring them into his active consciousness and enable him to guide others towards the same ideal.

The presence of Elias at the Transfiguration scene confirms the high state of spiritual evolution that Jesus had reached in his previous life as Elijah. However, as Moses was a prophet as well as a Messenger of God, he was necessarily an initiate of very high rank. Therefore he was qualified to be the invisible counsellor of Jesus, training and guiding him from the inner planes prior to his attainment of Christhood, after which the Celestial Christ became his source of inspiration, blessing and power. In all the greater initiations the Master who trains the candidate acts as his sponsor, and presents him when qualified to a senior hierophant, with the assurance that he is worthy of further advancement on the Path to God.

At this stage Luke states : " Peter and they that were with him were heavy with sleep," which is a simile employed to indicate that the vehicles of consciousness below the soul plane were necessarily quiescent. This state is confirmed by the additional phrase : " and when they were awake, they saw his glory," implying that as they had " ascended the mountain," that is to the planes of consciousness belonging to the higher self, they could perceive a glimpse of the effulgent light in the soul. Therefore, the remark ascribed to Peter, as being of no purpose, is really more profound in a mystical sense than the literal text suggests. It shows he was sufficiently advanced to realize there are higher faculties still awaiting development, and to these heights he and his companions aspired to reach. These correspond to the status of Elias, Jesus and Moses respectively, that is the heart, the soul and the spirit. As each one requires an appropriate vehicle of expression, it is essential that younger initiates should make every possible effort to develop, that is, to build, the requisite tabernacles.

The cloud that overshadowed the disciples at the climax of this vision is an allusion indicating that their range of perception, which was naturally restricted to their actual state of development, was limited. The following phrase :

" when they looked round about they saw no man
any more, save Jesus only, with themselves ;"

is quite in accord with this interpretation. It defines the condition of the individual who has been privileged to have such a blissful experience, and then " comes down the mountain " in order to resume the duties of his normal life in the world. Only he is no more a simple three dimensional personality, because he has become a kindled heart that is blessed by the light of the soul and the conscious presence of the Christ within. However, the " things they had seen " cannot be revealed to the ordinary man of the world, but only to those who have elevated their state of awareness to higher planes, which is implied in the words : " Until the son of man has risen from the dead," meaning one who is liberated from the bondage of mundane interests centralized in the lower self.

The fact that the " disciples questioned among themselves what this could mean," rather than inquire of Jesus, indicates that they had not actually experienced the ecstasy of Transfiguration within themselves.   They were being prepared for this high initiation by their Master, who therefore gave them this opportunity to witness its effect on himself, so that later they might be qualified to follow in his steps.   Such is the privilege that awaits all those who are ready to ascend the mountain in his company.

CHAPTER X

THE MARRIAGE IN CANA

Of the four Evangelists John is the only one who describes this remarkable story, which he records immediately after the Master appointed his disciples. Although Cana is generally presumed to have been a village in the district of Galilee, many authorities express serious doubts that there really existed such a country town during the lifetime of Jesus.

Cana means a " measuring rod " and suggests the channel through which the " soul energy of Galilee " found expression, enabling the Master to perform his most eminent miracles. Therefore, like the word Nazareth, it was probably introduced to give colour and deeper meaning to the story.

The setting of this narrative shows it is intended to be an allegory, which hides a deep spiritual experience rather than an unusual biographical incident, such as the words appear to imply. The account is couched in concise language and depicts a scene at a village marriage feast, in which the bride and bridegroom, and also the governor of the feast, are all referred to vaguely and in a distinctly impersonal manner.

Although it is said that the disciples were present, none of them takes any active part in the celebrations. Moreover, while it clearly stated that " the Mother of Jesus was there," her tentative effort to render some service evoked such a derogatory rebuke from her son, that it has caused much chagrin and incredulity on the part of his faithful followers. These ambiguous circumstances call for an impartial investigation. This may disclose whether there is a spiritual interpretation which will remove all perplexity and give further illumination to our understanding. It may also furnish another essential feature in this wonderful Drama of the Soul that is so carefully veiled, but which is the true spirit that underlies the literal text of the Gospels.

Let us adopt as our theorem the assumption that John really endeavoured to describe the indescribable. He certainly gave a graphic picture comprising the main features of the Mystical Marriage, this being the spiritual union of the human soul with the Divine Spirit. This is the true aim of man's highest aspirations, and it was frequently referred to in the ancient Mystery Rites of Egypt and Greece as the elevation of one's manhood into the Godhead. Therefore it is perfectly correct that it should have an important place in the Gospels.

Being the great Initiate and ideal Master of his age, Jesus was amply qualified to describe such an advanced stage of spiritual development. This exposition of the Marriage in Cana reveals a higher degree on the Path to God-realization than that attained either at the Baptism or at the Transfiguration. The Baptism describes the descent of the Holy Spirit, who is synonymous with the Celestial Christ and whose Light first illumines the soul of a high initiate. A further stage was revealed by the Transfiguration, when this illumination reaches its fullness. This corresponds to "entering the Kingdom of Heaven" and becoming a conscious Son of the Father. The next stage of the inner Teaching of Jesus was this mystical Marriage in Cana, which reveals the highest elevation of the human soul when the individual draws aside the veil of separation, and the sense of duality is first surmounted. In this exalted state he approaches human perfection. After this the Master still retained his human form in order to become a Messenger of God and so manifest "the Power and Glory of the Lord."

There is some danger of misunderstanding the nature of Christhood attained by an individual such as Jesus, and that of the Lord Christ. The latter is a real and vital, but celestial being who, having passed through all experiences possible in human form, advanced still further and became Living Light. In this capacity he embraces all humanity and thus he is the Mediator between the Father and mankind. His spiritual status and rank are beyond those of Jesus or any other human manifestation of Christhood. Actually he was the source of inspiration, illumination and revelation of the blessed Master, who continues to be a dynamic spiritual guide and font of benediction to mankind. The Celestial Christ is the supreme World Teacher, the Master of Masters and the guiding spirit behind all the great religions known to humanity. Therefore, each and every illumined Prophet who has brought a Message of God to mankind has been an embodiment and expression of the Celestial Christ, who in turn is fulfilling the Will of God, and so assisting the accomplishment of His Creative Plan.

There are several progressive stages in the spiritual development of the Prophet of Nazareth. The first grade was that of Jesus, when he was mystically re-born in the esoteric school of Bethlehem. The second degree was his attainment of Christhood at his Baptism in the Jordan, which is a metaphorical description of his being immersed by the influx of the Holy Spirit. The third stage was the Transfiguration, when he realized his immortal nature, perceived the mission he had to fulfil and also the consequences to be endured. A still higher degree was revealed in the perfecting of his human nature at the Marriage in Cana. This wonderfully sequential development and achievement is graphically recorded in the Gospel stories and makes Jesus Christ the outstanding figure in religious history.

John opens his narrative with the vague, yet truly significant words:

" And the third day there was a marriage in Cana of Galilee."

These Hebrew words furnish a key to the esoteric interpretation, for Cana implies : " a spiritual state of consciousness," while Galilee shows that this condition was suffused
with : " the energy and light of the soul," thus demonstrating
that it was a metaphysical and inner experience.

The text continues : " And the Mother of Jesus was there,"
which makes it appear to have been quite a normal and social
event.   However, there is no indication as to who were the
privileged couple, who should have been the principal
characters in this scene of the drama.   Really, the presence
of the Mother of Jesus supplements the mystical inference
of " Cana in Galilee," because she represents the intuitional
faculty of the candidate for this high manifestation, consequently she can only play a part of minor importance.

From the words that follow :

" And both Jesus was called, and his disciples, to
the marriage,"

we note that the Master is the only character who is specifically
referred to by name, which proves that he is intended to be the
central figure.   Jesus personifies the mystical heart with the
quality of love for all mankind, to which had been added the
consciousness of his innate Christhood.   Thus he represents
the awakened soul, who is the true psyche and the nameless
Bride awaiting the Bridegroom.

The unnamed disciples indicate his minor human faculties,
because his entire being must respond to the call of the soul
and participate in the consummation of this mystical marriage,
as it is the most advanced degree of spiritual experience that
man, while still an individual, can attain to.   There must be
complete self-surrender of the personality and also co-
operation of the individual soul with God, in order that there
may be perfect union of the human spirit with the Divine.

Those simple but significant words : " and the third day,"
shed much light on this subject, for they form part of the

sentence : " There was a marriage in Cana of Galilee."
The " third day " is a metaphorical reference to the third plane
of the higher self, which is the soul and represents the Bride.
So the three essential characters who must participate in the
nuptials were present : Mary, personifying the intuition,
Jesus, representing the devotion of the heart, and Christ,
symbolizing the illumined soul ; conjointly they await the
arrival of the Bridegroom, who is the human-divine Spirit.
How subtle is the figurative language now employed to present
the next act :

> " And when they wanted wine, the Mother of Jesus
> saith unto him, they have no wine."

The word " wine " is used as a symbol of divine life, in
contrast with water which pertains to physical life, for as the
earth becomes fertile with the addition of water, so the soul
is vivified by spiritual wine. Because the intuition, personified as Mary, signifies the portal of the inner Sanctuary,
she acts as the guardian on the threshold, but feels the lack
of spiritual sustenance as she cannot enter the Holy of Holies.
" Oh thou, who constantly reacheth upwards," is the prerogative of the soul, which ever seeks higher attainment and
yearns for the final consummation of Union with the human-
divine Spirit. Therefore Jesus Christ, as the illumined soul,
cannot look back, nor consider the behest of the lower faculties
which he has long surpassed. He has now only one more
stage of progress to achieve in order to attain human perfection,
so it is important he should remain resolute and steadfast to
the end. Hence we encounter his apparently disdainful and
incomprehensible rebuff :

> " And Jesus saith unto her, woman, what have I to do
> with thee ? mine hour is not yet come."

How graphic is the indication that this final stage of
spiritual development cannot be quickly accomplished.
Certainly it does not happen on the physical plane, not can it

be consummated within the space of an hour or two. It is the most arduous and anxious undertaking the human soul can ever experience, and only the Bridegroom, the Divine Spirit, knows when the soul is ready for this Mystical Union.

As the intuition constitutes the bridge between the higher self and the three-fold personality, and the latter is symbolized as the servants, it is quite appropriate that verse 5 records :

" His Mother saith unto the servants, whatsoever he saith unto you, do it."

It is imperative at this stage in the life of the advanced initiate that the entire conduct of life should be guided and directed from the high plane of the soul, and to her demand all the faculties of the lower self must be subservient.

The next verse presents a remarkably eloquent though metaphorical definition of what has been gradually taking place, but alas, its materialized and literal version has evoked endless queries.

" And there were set there six waterpots . . .containing two or three firkins apiece."

How astute was the writer in establishing exactly the requisite number of " six waterpots," and in definitely stating their size and capacity ! The word " firkin " is an old English standard measure comprising 9 gallons, or 56 lbs in weight. Verses 7-8 read :

" Jesus saith unto them, fill the waterpots with water. And they filled them to the brim. And he saith unto them, draw out now, and bear unto the governor of the feast. And they bare it."

How many scholars and students have been utterly perplexed by this statement and the incongruous situation which was thus presumably created by the Master, especially when it is interpreted as " the beginning of his miracles." To produce

miraculously, and thus provide over 400 pints of " good wine "
at the termination of a village wedding feast, would infer that
Jesus was himself a wine-bibber, and that he heartily encouraged heavy drinking, especially on such occasions.   This
indeed is the tragic conclusion derived from accepting " the
word that killeth " and ignoring the underlying " spirit that
giveth life," to which the Master called special attention.
How much dismay and despair have been caused by the
inappropriate and incorrect interpretation of this symbolic
phrase ! It should be an obvious allegory showing the
spiritual progress of the soul, with the first manifestation of its
conscious Christhood and the prelude to its At-one-ment
with The Father.

The veil of mystery that hides the most sacred event in the
entire career of the soul should now be drawn aside.   This
Marriage in Cana was not, and never could be, a profane
physical occurrence ; it was then, and ever must be, the most
holy and sublime spiritual experience that man can undergo.

The deeper significance of filling the waterpots is that they
symbolize the various bodies which the initiate has been so
laboriously building up during his long pilgrimage of earthly
existence.   The author is careful to indicate that each waterpot
represents the average weight of a man, that is 8 to 12 stone,
which is the equivalent of " 2 to 3 firkins apiece."   Therefore
they refer to the various vehicles of human consciousness :
the physical and emotional bodies, the concrete mind and
intuition together with the kindled heart and the illumined
soul.   In order to confirm this assumption and leave no doubt
as to its metaphysical meaning, the command is given :
" fill the waterpots with water " up to the brim.

As water symbolizes the ocean of human life, and there are
six bodies to be " filled," a fair inference is that the candidate
for this high spiritual manifestation must have had every
possible experience on all planes of his being.   Finally there
comes the process of transmuting the waters of life of

transient human existence into the " good wine " of transcendent spiritual being.   When this sublimation is accomplished, then every feature and faculty of the individual
becomes permeated with the Divine Presence, that is the good
wine left until the last.   Only the best and purest qualities
are worthy to be offered as a token of our homage and
gratitude to God.

The " Governor of the feast " is the divine Spirit of
Guidance who is ever watching us during our earthly life.
He must wait until each one of us fulfils our task of perfecting
all the different aspects of our nature, ranging from the
physical to the Spiritual.   When these become imbued with
the fruits of many long lives, fully and intensely lived so that
there is no looking back on unsatisfied desires, it may well be
said : " mine hour is come."   Then the Ruler of our earthly
feast will call us, and approve our labour in producing the
" good wine " of Love, Wisdom and Power at the end of our
human career.   The seal of perfection is when the entire
composite being is transmuted and divinized, so that " the
Soul can enter into the Glory of her Lord."   Thus " the
dewdrop slips into the Shining Sea ;" and Jesus manifests
his body of immortal bliss.

The earthly instrument then becomes a fit channel and
vehicle for divine manifestation, so that the human being may
be a Messenger of God.   Although he is " man in the form
of man, he is God in the consciousness of God."   It was this
supreme accomplishment that qualified the Master to be
recognized as : Jesus, Christ and The Lord, the embodiment
of human perfection.

In the verse that immediately follows this story John
furnishes a remarkable epilogue, the significance of which is
hidden in symbolic guise :

" After this he went down to Capernaum, he, and
his mother, and his brethren, and his disciples ;
and they continued there not many days."

The esoteric key is hidden in the words : " down to Capernaum," for " down " certainly implies a descent from a higher plane, and Capernaum means " a shelter of comfort and covering of compassion." Undoubtedly those who accompanied him in this exalted inner experience were his closest relatives and friends ; they personify his own individual faculties. These he must now carry back into earthly life, in order that he may become a Saviour of mankind and accomplish the mission that he voluntarily undertakes.

The soul who has attained the state of Christhood, and also merged his being into the divine Spirit, has become so delicately attuned and spiritualized that he must suffer extreme mental anguish and physical agony, by returning to worldly existence. To be surrounded by gross vibrations, that are charged with the selfishness, hatred and malice of mundane life, wounds every fibre of his refined constitution. Therefore does he need divine benediction and the shield of spiritual Light, which will provide him with a " shelter of comfort and a covering of compassion," for this is a Master's prerogative.

So much superlative wisdom is revealed in this apparently simple verse that it constitutes the crowning climax to a spiritual allegory that is unique in sacred literature.

How profoundly illumined was the original author of this wonderful story. Who else could have recounted it with all its mystery and subtle symbolism, other than Jesus Christ himself ! He was the only person of his epoch to have such a supernal experience, and he left this sublime record for our guidance so that we might follow in his steps.

CHAPTER XI

In all the world's literature there is no more tragic and touching scene than the Crucifixion of Jesus. The graphic records of the Gospels have made a more profound appeal to the heart of mankind than the martyrdom and suffering of any other individual in history.

Why should this be so ? Have there not been many instances of heinous atrocity and callous cruelty perpetrated against other innocent individuals, whose protracted pain and agonizing tortures may have far exceeded all that which was imposed upon the Prophet of Nazareth ? Is it only because he is the central figure of Christendom that the memory of his terrible end has been constantly recounted in such moving terms ? Surely there is another factor of deeper and more universal significance than the solemn and supremely sublime self-sacrifice of his gracious person. The mystical fact is that his pathetic figure on the Cross of Calvary represents the final scene in this Drama of the Soul, in which every human being must eventually assume a corresponding part.

If we condense the four Gospels into one composite narrative it will be found that practically all the extraordinary details of his life have two meanings, the biographical and the spiritual. But the latter interpretation reveals features of far greater importance than the historical events that preceded the end of his mission in Palestine. Although the agony on Golgotha represents the climax of this moving story, the Garden of Gethsemane presents an eloquent prologue to show the mental anguish caused by the unavoidable surrender of all that is held most dear in human life, whereas the Resurrection and Ascension describe an epilogue overflowing with the glorious recompense of ecstatic joy and peace that surpass man's highest dreams of worldly happiness.

Having analysed the most conspicuous episodes in the earlier stages of the soul's pilgrimage, as portrayed by the inner life of Jesus, we are better qualified to understand and appreciate his final and most crucial experiences. The importance of this narrative lies in the fact that it reveals what each one of us must endure, before we can attain conscious Union with The Father, by merging our human nature into the Divine Godhead. This is the mystery and ideal underlying the Crucifixion.

THE PASSOVER

Matthew XXVI, 2, states :

> " Ye know that after two days is the feast of the passover, and the son of man is betrayed to be crucified."

Why should this tragic portent be introduced by the words : " after two days," if not to show that when the dual nature of man, physical and spiritual, is completely developed, there must come the final passing over of all that which was human in order that it may be reintegrated into the Divine Being. This subtle introduction of the Passover has been little understood, but it is of extreme importance because there are recorded three progressive degrees which, despite their historical aspects, have also profound mystical significance. To " pass over " means to overcome any obstruction or impediment on the Path that leads to God. In this light to " pass over the Red Sea," which assured the liberation of the Israelites from their bondage in Egypt, should be interpreted as the first stage, as it symbolizes man's release from the coils of excessive emotionalism and sensual passion. Later there

THE 7 CHAKRAS ɪɴ ETHERIC BODY

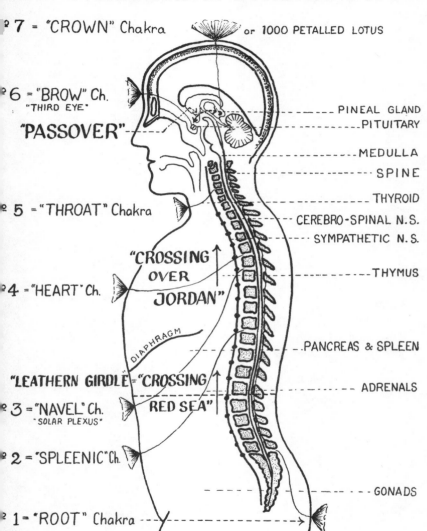

7 = "CROWN" Chakra — or 1000 PETALLED LOTUS

6 = "BROW" Ch.
"THIRD EYE"

"PASSOVER"

PINEAL GLAND
PITUITARY
MEDULLA
SPINE
THYROID

5 = "THROAT" Chakra

CEREBRO-SPINAL N.S.
SYMPATHETIC N.S.

"CROSSING ↑
OVER
JORDAN"

THYMUS

4 = "HEART" Ch.

DIAPHRAGM

PANCREAS & SPLEEN

"LEATHERN GIRDLE" = "CROSSING ↑
RED SEA"

ADRENALS

3 = "NAVEL" Ch.
"SOLAR PLEXUS"

2 = "SPLEENIC" Ch.

GONADS

1 = "ROOT" Chakra

follows the crossing of the river Jordan under the guidance of Joshua, in order to " pass over " into the Promised Land. This denotes man's progress on the Path by elevating his consciousness into the planes of the higher self, and it is a precedent to " entering the Kingdom of Heaven." But the third phase of the Passover is far more abstruse, and a fuller analysis of the stages of the Crucifixion will disclose how skilfully disguised is this final transmutation of man's human nature, in order that it may partake of the consciousness of the Divine Presence.

The first significant act in this dramatic story presents Jesus in a house in Bethany, when :

> " a woman having an alabaster box of precious ointment poured it on his head as he sat at meat,"

and Jesus said it should " be told for a memorial of her." In a literal sense such an action seems hardly credible, nor is the purpose of perpetuating her memory quite obvious. There-fore we must assume that the account is incorporated into the text in order to convey some deeper teaching. First it is noted that the word " Bethany " means : " house of affliction or distress," and it also implies " a place where crossings are made ;" both these ideas are appropriately relevant in the story. John, XI, 2, states : " It was that Mary which anointed the Lord," and this sister of Lazarus is depicted as an embodiment of selfless devotion. The " precious ointment " is analogous to " burning incense," and therefore is a fit symbol of rendering homage and worship to God. So this incident may be interpreted as indicating that the aspirant, personified as Jesus, dedicates himself with undeviating con-stancy to the ideal of attainment he has envisaged. This can be consummated by means of " affliction and crossing over " which are subsidiary features in the tragedy of the Crucifixion, the inner purport of which is disclosed by subsequent events.

The act of homage performed by Mary, indicating the intuition, " while he sat at meat," means that he gave freely of his spiritual teaching in the service of God and mankind.

> " When the disciples saw it they had indignation, saying to what purpose is this waste ? For the ointment might have been sold for much, and given to the poor."

Jesus perceived their doubts came from the lower faculties, therefore he answered :

> " Why trouble ye the woman, for she has wrought a good work upon me. For ye have the poor always with you ; but me ye have not always."

First, the contrast between the two points of view is accentuated, for whereas the lower self may think devotion to an ideal is a waste of time and energy, the higher self,—comprising the intuition, heart and soul, and corresponding to Mary, Jesus and the Christ,—understands that by thinking of God one becomes God-like. Although the emphasis on the " poor " seems to imply indigent people, the Master evidently considered those people are really poor who do not understand the purpose and beauty of life. His further remark that : " she did it for my burial," demonstrates that to give openly from the heart is the surest and simplest method of self-effacement, which is the requisite attitude for the aspirant who is preparing for this inner experience of self-surrender. These Christ Doctrines are perforce deeply veiled, but may be rightly understood and applied by mature souls, or when the appropriate time approaches in life to follow in the steps of the Master.

Now there is introduced the character of Judas, the base individual who betrayed his Master. He represents in man the " uncontrolled generative desire nature and covetousness," while Iscariot means : " a man of the cities, and a worldly individual of hostile encounters." Moreover, it is said Judas " was a thief " because he robs the soul of its rightful inheritance, therefore he betrays the Christ principle.

What is the inference of the words : " for thirty pieces of silver ?" As thirty combines three times ten, and this latter number is a cypher indicating the aggregation of experiences on any plane of consciousness, " thirty " denotes the three lower bodies of the personality. This deduction is confirmed by the word " silver," because it symbolizes a mere reflection such as moonlight, and does not represent the source of living light, as that which comes from the sun. So, by analogy, the lower ego only reflects the light of the soul ; but it is always working in opposition to the soul in its effort to fulfil its destiny by achieving liberation from worldly bondage.

Again, in his fugal method of tuition, the Master reaffirms this fact by stating :

" He that dippeth his hand with me in the dish, the
same shall betray me,"

because the personal self only partakes of physical food in preference to spiritual sustenance. This latter aspect is now adroitly presented in order to emphasize the contrast between the natures of Judas and Jesus :

" And he took bread, and blessed it and brake it, and
gave it to his disciples."

This is a figurative description of expounding his inner doctrines. To " break bread " suggests revealing divine wisdom regarding the purpose and destiny of human life, while his blood symbolizes the essence of love which he manifested so ardently.

What is implied by the guest chamber which Luke describes with such mysterious detail ? The two disciples who were sent to prepare the Passover were Peter, who represents enlightened understanding and faith, with John, who personifies the Love quality. They were to " enter into the city," such as the mind with its concourse of thoughts and ideas. There they would meet : " a man bearing a pitcher of water," which symbolizes the higher reasoning faculty and intuition. This man would " lead them into a house," meaning the kindled heart ; and the owner thereof would show them : " a large upper room, furnished," indicating the soul.

The highest plane of human consciousness, and the only one where this " great renunciation " can take place, is the soul. It is there that " the passover," or " pascal lamb must be eaten," implying that the entire selfhood of the aspirant has to be purified and transformed ; hence every disciple must participate in the " last supper." All this descriptive scenery represents a prologue to the more tragic scenes that follow, because the Garden of Gethsemane, the Judgement Hall and Golgotha are all symbolical aspects of the inner nature of the one who is preparing for this final initiation.

The text continues : " when they had sung a hymn ;" this indicates a further expression of devotion, which is confirmed by the words : " Mount of Olives." This phrase designates : " a luminous principle and exalted enlighten- ment," that is the high plane of consciousness maintained while he continues to expound the mysteries of the Kingdom of Heaven, and simultaneously prepares for his own coming ordeal. It should be noted that the word : " disciples " is also employed with a dual meaning, because it signifies not only his closest pupils and friends, but also his own lower faculties. As he is now functioning from the plane of the soul, he addresses them :

> " Ye shall be offended with me this night, because it is written I will smite my shepherd (himself), and the sheep (his disciples) shall be scattered."

How ingenious is the introduction of this portent in order to show that Peter, symbolizing the concrete mind and vacilla- ting faith of a young aspirant, assures his Master of loyalty and co-operation, whereas Jesus, with his penetrating insight and wisdom, affirms that :

> " this night, before the cock crows twice thou shalt deny me thrice."

This cryptic phrase implies that during the darkness of ignorance the lower self cannot understand the nature and destiny of the soul, but right perception will surely come with the dawn of a new day when a higher stage of unfoldment is attained.

Remarkably illuminating omens are portrayed when :

> " Jesus rode into Jerusalem seated on an ass, and the multitude cried saying, Hosanna to the son of David."

The " ass " was regarded as a " bearer of royalty," a " king " implies one who has attained perfection, " Jerusalem " means : " the abode of peace," and " Hosanna " signifies : " save now, seek liberation now." So again we see how astutely certain historical aspects are combined with spiritual features in the mystical life of the Master.

GETHSEMANE

This drama now presents a scene of the saddest and most touching pathos as it reveals the necessity for absolute renunciation of all worldly ties.

> " Then cometh Jesus with them unto a place called Gethsemane, and he said unto his disciples, sit ye here. And he took with him Peter, James and John."

They were the same friends, or faculties, that accompanied him at his Transfiguration, when he was shown a vision of what is now actually coming to pass.

> " Then saith he unto them, my soul is exceeding sorrowful, even unto death. Tarry ye here and watch with me ; and he went a little further and prayed."

Here is to be noted the foreboding of his self-surrender, to accomplish which he must elevate his consciousness beyond that of his " disciples." Although he is functioning as an illumined soul, he has not yet liberated himself from the grip of self-hood. So he must face the terrible ordeal of definitely renouncing every vestige of the individuality, and all that has been so zealously built up during past ages and by innumerable incarnations.

How carefully the necessary Hebrew words were compiled and chosen, and then given the most appropriate setting in order to enhance every fact and feature of this excruciating experience. Although Gethsemane implies the garden of sorrow and affliction, its actual meaning is " the oil press," such as is used to extract the essence of all that is of value. Metaphorically, it casts aside all useless residue, because only that which is pure and perfect can be sublimated and then offered to the Father as the harvest of earthly toil, tribulation and triumph. So the initiate who is advancing towards human perfection must leave behind all the dross and debris of the personal equation. Hence the purposeful words :

> " Tarry ye here and watch with me, while I go and
> pray yonder. O my Father, if it be possible, let this
> cup pass from me."

This entreaty accentuates how difficult it is to subjugate the inferior elements of the self. The soul knows it must accomplish its pre-ordained work, for the Creative Plan cannot be ignored or evaded. Therefore Jesus reluctantly offers to renounce all : " Not as I will, but as Thou wilt." Even so, the task seems almost insuperable, for " He cometh unto his disciples, (his lower faculties), and finding them asleep " to these high spiritual realities.

> " **What, could ye not watch with me one brief hour ?
> The spirit is indeed willing, but the flesh is weak.**"

Not yet is the battle won, for :

> " He went a second and third time and prayed,
> saying, O my Father, if this cup may not pass from
> me, except I drink it, Thy Will be done."

The dreadful desolation of this struggle between the ties of physical self-hood and the soul's quest for liberation must be borne in utter loneliness, for the final self-effacement must be entirely voluntary, and the imperative decision must be taken without help or persuasion from others.

> " And he came and found them asleep again, for
> their eyes were heavy."

Even God Himself will not deprive the individual of his free-will, for he must : " choose the good and refuse the evil," lest this great sacrifice lose its value and virtue.   So in grim solitude he makes the stern resolve :

> " Rise, let us be going, behold he is at hand that doth
> betray me."

In such terms is this agonizing ordeal dramatized.   It was and ever must be an inner and individual conflict, and the conquest can only be achieved in solitude by one's own courage and decision, and when seemingly abandoned by one's most intimate companions and colleagues : "For all the disciples forsook him and fled."   It is said : " Peter followed him afar off," because faith, coupled with the reasoning mind, cannot accompany the soul when it utters the inevitable verdict of final self-surrender.

Another significant scene in the Garden of Gethsemane is enacted when Judas and the multitude went to arrest Jesus :

> " Peter drew his sword and struck a servant of the
> high priest and smote off his ear."

Why should this incident be recorded ?   Is it not to show that as soon as it was evident that the Jews had rejected Jesus, Peter, as the principal disciple, sought to deprive them of the

privilege of hearing any more of his Teaching ?   But not so
the Master, for :   " until seventy times seven he forgives ;"
moreoever :

> " He came to call sinners to repentance."
> " Therefore said he, put up thy sword into its place."

How true his axiom has since proved :   " all they that take
the sword shall perish by the sword."   The drama further
unfolds :

> " And they that had laid hold of Jesus led him away to
> Caiaphas."

The name of this high priest means :   " hollowed out, a
depression," which is supplemented by the : "ruling power
of religious thought that is entirely intellectual and subject
to form and ceremony, but without spiritual illumination."
No wonder he misunderstood the Master and resented his
wider spiritual Teaching.   Even Peter could only : " sit by
the door with the servants," indicating that the intellect is
bound to the inferior faculties, and so remains mute and
disconsolate outside the portal of the inner temple wherein
resides the spirtual illumination of Christ-consciousness.

Only false and worldly witnesses can be found to criticize
and clamour against the irrevocable career of the soul.   So
few can understand the mystical necessity of destroying the
last remaining elements of the egocentric personality, which
does not wish to acknowledge it is a temple of God.   The
Father can only assume His rightful prerogative, and make
His abode within our souls, when we empty ourselves of all
thought of self ; but how painful and protracted is this
process ! To " rebuild the temple in three days " is a
veiled allusion to the essential spiritualization of the three
higher bodies, and during this inner transformation it can
" answer nothing " against the false and cynical charges of
earth-bound people.   Only with unfeigned reluctance does
Jesus acknowledge his own great attainment when :

> " the high priest said unto him, I adjure thee by the
> living God, that thou tell us whether thou be the
> Christ, the son of God."

Such a high state of illumination was far beyond the comprehension even of the high priest, who said :

> " he hath spoken blasphemy ; what think ye ?
> They answered and said he is guilty of death."

This is a covert allusion to the mystical crisis that now awaits
him.   To add to his ignominy Peter denies that he even knew
Jesus :

> " Then the Lord looked upon him, and immediately
> the cock crew,"

showing that only with further development can one understand the Master's Teaching.   " Then he went out and wept
bitterly."   Even so, he had not the courage or confidence to
stand by his friend in his greatest peril.   But Judas, representing the lowest elements of the personal self, recants
and acknowledges that :   " I have sinned and betrayed
innocent blood."

There follows the curious decision made by the high priests
to employ the rejected " thirty pieces of silver " in order to
purchase " the potter's field to bury strangers in. " This
seems a strange interjection in such a tragic theme.   However,
as a potter makes earthly forms, it suggests one who may
train young human beings, the field being his zone of activity.
As silver only reflects the light of truth, it suggests that the
orthodoxy which could not accept or recognize the Christ
Doctrines might serve as elementary teaching for strangers,
those in the " outer court," or lower self, although they would
be " buried " thereunder.

Jesus then stands in the judgement hall before the governor
Pilate, whose name signifies : " armed with a sword."   He
personifies earthly power and personal will, one who resents

any attempt to usurp his power, even though spiritually justified.   Symbolically the judgement hall is the three-fold lower self, and Pilate represents the desire of the ego which struggles to maintain supreme dominion over the entire being of man.   Recognizing the futility of argument, Jesus refuses to defend himself against external attacks and accusations, for Pilate said :

> " Thine own nation and the chief priests have delivered thee unto me. Hearest thou not how many things they witness against thee ?"

Despite the minor faculties of human nature that seek to frustrate the incessant urge of the soul in its anxious quest for liberation, it must remain steadfast, albeit silent.

At this juncture there is introduced a statement that most scholars deny as being historically true :

> " for of necessity Pilate must release one prisoner unto them at the feast of the Passover, whomsoever they will."

Some writers allege that by this means the guilt of condemning the Master was transferred from Rome to Judah.   But there is another and far more subtle aspect that is rarely referred to, perhaps because it is purposely obscure and has been introduced with a spiritual objective.   The mystical truth is that the inner process which is to be consummated by the Crucifixion is to reach the apex of human existence, and this means liberating the soul itself, for it has been long imprisoned in physical form.   A strange but confirmatory statement is made by the Jews :

> " we have a law that he should die, because he made himself a Son of God ; "

this is the metaphorical death of the individual self so that the soul can be " released."   Therefore Jesus reveals this mystery by demonstrating how the requisite freedom is to be given to the " prisoner." There is purposeful emphasis laid on the words attributed to Pilate :

> " Whom will ye that I release unto you, Barabbas or Jesus who is called Christ, for he knew that for envy they had delivered him ; and from thenceforth Pilate sought to release him."

In this quandary his wife cautions him saying :

> " Have thou nothing to do with this just man, for I have suffered many things this day in a dream because of him."

Again there is presented the inner conflict between the lower and the higher mind. Pilate excuses himself by making Jesus acknowledge he is " King of the Jews," and consequently he might create insurrection against Roman law and order. But the Master gives the appropriate definition of his true status :

> " My kingdom is not of this world, but to this end I was born into the world that I might bear witness of the Truth."

Then Pilate said unto the Jews : " I find in him no fault at all ; behold your king !" In an esoteric sense the title of " king " means one who has attained perfection. But the people clamoured :

> " deliver unto us Barabbas, . . . now Barabbas was a notable prisoner who had committed murder."

Some stigma is hidden in his name, for *Bar* means son, and *Abbas* is " father or spiritual teacher," hence he was only a son, or pupil. Therefore to liberate such a criminal among the people in preference to the illumined Prophet, implies that the " chief priests persuaded the multitude " to accept a travesty of half truths.

Then followed the odious scene of scorn and derison, when the soldiers :

> " put on him a scarlet robe, . . . a crown of thorns
> on his head, and a reed in his right hand ; and they
> bowed the knee before him, and mocked him."

All these gestures reflect cynical sarcasm, because they really symbolize the royal estate of Christhood, which neither they nor the high priests could understand or appreciate. The " crown of thorns " is especially graphic because it reflects the mental agony of disappointment, delusion and despair caused by the criticism and condemnation of worldly men and their rejection of his Message. All this animosity must be borne in silence by the seeker after God.

It is said that Jesus fell under the weight of the Cross, which implies that when the physical body predominates it drags the soul down. A different phase is astutely presented by : " compelling Simon the Cyrenean to carry the cross," as these names indicate that it is the " fixed state of thoughts and formal religious ideas " that should be crucified !

> " And as they led him away there followed a great
> company of people who bewailed and lamented him.
> And Jesus said, daughters of Jerusalem weep not for
> me, but for yourselves and your children."

He could then foresee the catastrophic destruction of their city when : " there shall not be left here one stone upon another," for practically all Christians abandoned the city in A.D. 66, and Jerusalem was destroyed four years later. Was this precipitated by the sinister indifference of those who said to Pilate " let his blood be on our heads and on our children ?"

A further example of extreme subtlety that is veiled in the choice of words is the statement :

> " When they were come to a place called Golgotha,
> that is to say the place of the skull."

To give this meaning so clearly in the text should elicit our

investigation, because it is meant to emphasize that the
" mystical crucifixion " actually takes place within the human
skull, as it is an inner spiritual experience, when the limited
individual consciousness is finally surrendered to God.   The
fact that Golgotha was located : " just outside Jerusalem" is
a veiled indication that the " abode of peace " is within reach
of the initiate.

It is is recorded that :

> " They parted my garments among them, and upon
> my vesture did they cast lots."

This division of the clothing of Jesus is generally interpreted
quite literally, but the esoteric version conveys ideas of a more
profound nature.   John states that because :

> " the coat was without seam, woven from the top
> throughout they said, let us not rend it."

The word " garments " is a fitting analogy for the doctrines
of Jesus, which were later so regrettably subdivided amongst
different groups and diverse cults that evince little desire to
reunite the " four parts " into their original completion.
That which is " woven from the top throughout " is an
eloquent definition of the Teaching he gave of spiritual
evolution and its ultimate perfection of Christhood.   This
cannot be rent asunder, because once it is understood it
reveals every requisite step towards human liberation.   But
so little has this tuition been understood or esteemed by the
" soldiers," who represent the guardians of the scriptures,
that it has fallen into the possession of a few outside gnostics
and mystics, and they rightly treasure it as " the pearl of great
price."

There are further passages in this tragic story, the meaning
of which is deeply disguised : " Father forgive them, for they
know not what they do."   Was this appeal uttered merely on
behalf of those who were directly responsible for his Crucifixion, and not for those who have perversely misunderstood

him and betrayed his innermost doctrines ?   He was speaking
as the Messenger sent for the Piscean era to give Teaching
which was then, and has ever since been rejected by the
majority.   No religious teacher has been so sadly traduced as
Jesus, and no spiritual teaching so perversely travestied as the
Christ Doctrines !

> " Then were there two thieves crucified with him,
> one on the right hand and another on the left."

In a mystical sense, when an initiate is undergoing this
" great renunciation," not only is the body crucified, but also
the emotional nature and the lower mind, for these two
faculties have constantly robbed the soul of its divine birth-
right of spiritual life and light.   That form of conduct which
was permissible in the preliminary stages of human evolution
must later be repressed or purified, with the progress of
civilization and altruistic culture.   However, the egoistic
desire nature is indifferent and without remorse, therefore :

> " he railed on him saying, if thou be the Christ, save
> thyself and us."

But the other malefactor, the reasoning faculty, dimly discerns
the irrevocable course of human destiny, and :—

> " rebuked him, saying, dost thou not fear God, seeing
> thou art in the same condemnation, (as the physical
> body), but we indeed justly receive the due reward
> of our deeds ; but this man has done nothing amiss.
> And he said unto Jesus, Lord, remember me when
> thou comest into thy kingdom.   And Jesus said unto
> him, verily today thou shalt be with me in Paradise."

The true individuality of the soul has hitherto been covered,
and merely reflected on the mind which has been mostly
interested and involved in mundane affairs.   Now the rational
intelligence becomes purged and transmuted into wise understanding of spiritual principles, and can function in higher
realms.

The first three hours of agony on the cross may be thus symbolized : thy hands are nailed for thou shalt cease from all desire of self-defence ; thy feet are pinioned, for thou must suspend all activity for thine own welfare ; and thy heart is pierced, for there can be no more love of self ! These three crucified figures are a variation of Daniel's friends who were cast into the fiery furnace, whence arose a fourth and radiant being, symbolizing the spiritualization of human nature into its inherent divinity. Certainly there were illuminated souls in those days who knew these inner mysteries of life. The records of the Nazarene's initiations are like " Ezekiel's roll, written within and without," for they are more spiritual than literal in their meaning.

Another utterance from the cross is cited only by John, perhaps because he *lived the part* as presented, when Jesus said :

" Woman behold thy son, and then turned to the
disciple whom he loved, saying, behold thy mother."

Surely, too limited is the assumption that the Master was only making John responsible for the future welfare of Mary, laudable though such an idea may be. We are witnessing a spiritual drama in which every scene and act has its rightful place and purpose. Through those two personalities the Master was really addressing the feminine intuition of mankind, because the faculty of the higher self is invariably awakened by personal suffering, and thence is born the kindled heart of love and sympathy that corresponds to Jesus ; this stage was then being attained by " the beloved disciple." Only by such successive steps can be realized the illumination of Christhood, so clearly revealed in the Master's assurance : " I, if I be lifted up, will lift all men unto me." How earnestly he sought to reveal the underlying purpose of life, and also to show us the best means to accomplish our pre-ordained destiny.

This drama now discloses a more poignant picture, deftly
veiled under cypher and symbol :

> " Now from the sixth hour there was darkness over
> the land until the ninth hour."

What has *time* to do with the eternal nature of the soul ? So
naïvely have these words been construed that some people
believe an eclipse of the sun then occurred, in order to
demonstrate divine disapproval of the murder of the " Only
Begotten Son." This time factor, from mid-day to three p.m.,
was merely employed to indicate the transformation that is
unfolding to the inner vision of the initiate. His threefold
personality is the real mystical cross upon which his soul hangs
impaled and helpless, for the final scenes of these crucial
experiences are only perceived by the soul. Hitherto it has
enjoyed the bliss of illumination coming from the " overshadowing Christ," but this privilege must now be withdrawn
in order that the initiate himself may become " a Christ."
It is this absence of the inner Light from the Celestial Christ
that is referred to as " darkness over the whole land," which
evokes the cry of anguish and despair, translated as : " my
God, why hast Thou forsaken me ?" As God is Omnipresent,
how can He forsake anyone ? We all live and move and have
our being in Him, though there are degrees of man's power to
perceive and appreciate the Divine Presence, which this Drama
of the Soul clearly reveals.

John most aptly states :

> " And it was the preparation of the passover, and
> about the sixth hour, and he saith unto the Jews,
> behold your King."

All these ideas substantiate the mystical truth that is now being
enacted. Observe the conjoint reference to the " preparation
of the passover," that is, the ultimate stage of passing from
manhood to God-realization ; the " sixth hour " precedes
7th and final act of surrender ; and : " behold your King "

describes the highest degree of initiation that is about to be realized.

Now we become more deeply immersed in mystery, firstly because this " cry from the cross " is transcribed literally from the Psalms. Moreover, there are several other statements attributed to Jesus, but which were evidently written a thousand years previously by his royal predecessor, and these are all recorded in the Psalms, for example :

> " They divided my garments among them, and upon my vesture did they cast lots."
> " They gave me gall for my meat, and in my thirst they gave me vinegar to drink."
> " They that sat at the gate speak against me."
> (This is a paraphrase of Peter's denial.)

Of far greater importance is : " They pierced my hands and feet," for surely David was not crucified !
> " He trusted in the Lord that He would deliver him ; let Him deliver him."

Finally, " Into Thy hands I commit my spirit."

In view of the above citations we must seriously question whether David himself did not also undergo similar mystical experiences to those described in the Crucifixion of Jesus, although he may not have reached the final phase. Some medical men doubt whether the mere piercing of hands and feet of a strong man would have fatal results within a few hours. Certain historians affirm that the form of the cross used by the Romans was in the shape of the capital letter " T ", and that the victim's arms were tied over the cross-bar ; he was often left in agony for 40 to 50 hours before death released him. It was not until A.D. 680 that Pope Adrian decreed that the figure of a man should be fixed to the cross ; thereafter this form was adopted as the Christian emblem of the vicarious sacrifice. In a metaphysical sense it is the human body that constitutes the real crucifix upon which the soul is transfixed, hence the spiritual ideal is to " release this prisoner." The cross was regarded as a mystical symbol ages before the birth of Jesus, for it represents two divergent currents of force, the upright signifying the descent of Divine Life into corporate form and of spirit into matter, whereas the cross-bar indicates the obstructions caused by human limitations and personal will, which separate man from God.

As the symbol of the cross is traced back into the past, all signs of suffering disappear and it becomes an emblem of the joyous giving of life and an expression of divine love through the outstretched hands in blessing.

In contrast with the anguish expressed by David, Matthew says :

> " Jesus cried with a loud voice, saying Eli, Eli, Lama Sabachthani, that is to say, My God, my God, why hast Thou forsaken me ?"

Many theologians have questioned the origin and meaning of this exclamation. The first word *Eli* is definitely Hebrew, and is translated as : " apex and most high," but " My Lord" would be a more appropriate interpretation, for it can scarcely be an appeal to the Absolute and Omnipresent God. Evidently it refers to the Celestial Christ, who was the main source of inspiration and power that Jesus manifested during his three years mission in Palestine. The real Christ is a Celestial Being, whereas Jesus was the human who elevated and expanded the range of his consciousness, so that he was able to reach up to the place and abode of The Christ, and thus consciously receive and transmit the special Christ Doctrines for the Western World. They are still two separate beings, although they work in close collaboration, but while Jesus is primarily engaged in guiding all Christians to a fuller understanding and a more spiritual application of his Teaching, the Celestial Christ is responsible for the promulgation of *all* religous doctrines in the world. Every true form of religion is a path that leads man God-wards, and it is this truth that justifies the Unity of Religious Ideals and World Brotherhood, because this is the great work that the Celestial Christ is promoting.

It will be recalled that at the time of the Baptism it is said : " The Holy Ghost descended upon Jesus ;" now, at this juncture of this Crucifixion, the records state :

> " When Jesus had cried with a loud voice, he yielded up the Ghost."

It is therefore obvious that what was conferred upon him when he was about 30 years of age was the supplement of Christhood, which endowed him with the faculty of universal consciousness, whereby his compass of vision and perception greatly surpassed that of other people. Despite the general assumption, there is no logical evidence to show that the words : " he yielded up the Ghost," are intended to mean that he then *died*, and the fact that it is explicitly stated : " he cried with a loud voice," indicates that in a physical sense he was still in virile good health, although the inference is that he was suffering inexpressible grief. In its mystical interpretation this act leads to the climax of the highest spiritual initiation that one can experience while still retaining the separate consciousness of a human being, and prior to merging into the God-head. The allegorical exposition is so skilfully designed that it requires close examination in order to understand all that is expressed, as well as that which is implied.

The word *Lama* is the same as that employed in Tibet ; it means a spiritual Head and Leader, and therefore confirms that it was addressed to the Lord Christ. The last composite word of this agonizing cry, *Sa-bach-thani*, comprises three words derived from the Hebrew, Greek and Arabic, and it is obviously a mystical cryptogram. The literal meaning is :

" Thy Celestial Light is extinguished within my soul, it is as death to me !"

The human individual Jesus was in a state of transition, and could not perceive all that was transpiring within his innermost being, nor the state of ecstatic joy that was then reserved for him. In an esoteric sense he was able to exercise the fullest faculties of the pituitary bodies, whereas the pineal gland and crown chakra were only temporarily stimulated by the Christ Presence, whose radiant power was reflected on to the pituitary centre. The trained seer and occultist may feel, or even see, this inner process as flashes of light, passing between these two centres when they are not functioning as a duad, but later they will unite and generate the highest illumination known as the " thousand petalled lotus." All this occurs between the two hemispheres of the brain, within the skull, hence the term Golgotha is quite justified. But in order that the pineal centre may be awakened, and so exercise its own inherent faculty, the overshadowing influence of the Celestial Christ must first be withdrawn, and there is a corresponding inner demand that the initiate must " yield up the Ghost," in order that " Thy Will be done." Because this temporary lack of inner illumination gives a sense of being abandoned and utterly alone, it is said : " there was darkness over the whole land," that is, the entire consciousness of the individual feels that : " Thy Light is extinguished within me." After this :

> " Jesus knowing that all things were now accomplished, and that the scriptures (the Divine Plan) might be fulfilled,"

uttered the yearning appeal for higher Spiritual Light and nurture : " I thirst !" There is no time factor in spiritual realms of consciousness, but only a definite sequence of events and progressive stages of unfoldment.

Now the text furnishes the most revealing clue to this mystery :

> " And the veil of the temple was rent in twain, from
> top to bottom."

The real Temple of God is the being of man, but while he is travelling on the Path and developing his human faculties he feels separated from the Father, and this causes the sense of duality and loneliness. " Lift the barrier between Thee and me, O Lord." So we are shown in this supreme act of the drama that the last remaining veil of obstruction is " rent in twain." This reveals the Holy of Holies, the Living Light of the human-divine Spirit, to his inner vision and gives him complete and independent illumination.

Now the fullest and final meaning of the cryptic cry is understood, and he exclaims with ecstatic joy :

> " Into Thy hands I commend my spirit ;—My Lord,
> my God, how Thou hast glorified me !"

He is no longer a separate and limited human being, because he is now " At-one with the Father," Therefore it was possible to declare : " truly this was the son of God." " Son of man " was a title given to an initiate on the Path, whereas " Son of God " is one who is perfected and liberated. " By losing all, he gains All." Then in his triumph of completing the final " Passover " he declares that the great work of the soul is accomplished ; truly " *It is finished*."

CHAPTER XII

From the foregoing mystical interpretation of the fourth great initiation of Jesus, it should not be assumed that there was no crucifixion on the physical plane ; on the contrary, he undoubtedly suffered martyrdom at the hands of those who misunderstood him and feared his Teaching would endanger their own prestige and power. But it will be recognized that as " God is Love " there could never be a divine decree secretly obliging anyone to commit an atrocity in order to establish a vicarious atonement that would be operative in " saving " others for innumerable centuries still to come.

This dogma has been incomprehensible and incredible to most people, and it has sadly obscured the real mystery and purpose of the final " Passover," for the Cross on Calvary was only a dim external reflection of the internal suffering that must be endured on superphysical planes, when the limited human individual is surrendered and the soul returns and reunites with the Universal Being.

The truth is that : " the cross upon Golgotha will never save my soul, until the cross within my heart leads me to the Goal." This is confirmed by the Master's urgent appeal : " Take up thy cross and follow me," in order to liberate the soul from its long imprisonment in human form. There can be no attainment of Christhood without the inner and mystical crucifixion.

There is a growing conviction that Jesus *did not die* on the cross. In comparatively recent times a nun who was renowned for her devotion to the Master was, at her own request, nailed to a recumbent wooden cross, and thus remained impaled for 6 hours, on eleven successive Good Fridays ; she did not die as a result thereof.

An erroneous idea was current in the early centuries of this era that a corpse could be miraculously resuscitated, and as the deeper meaning of the Crucifixion was not then generally understood, it was assumed that Jesus suffered death on the cross. Hence there was propounded the dogma of the Resurrection of his physical body, which was subsequently elevated into space ; this was taught without any logical consideration of what good purpose it could thus serve.

Such notions are no proof of divinity, they merely reflect immature understanding and materialization of mystical principles. They have had the regrettable effect of entirely obscuring the underlying mystery of man's spiritual evolution. Our innate divine nature will be restituted by the illumination and liberation of the soul, which must eventually be transmuted and elevated into transcendental realms and so dwell in the Presence of God.

In the course of human progress the threefold personality must be fully developed and exercised in order that all man's faculties may become inherent or active qualities. Then, prior to the first great initiation, corresponding to the second birth, it is necessary to practise self-discipline in order to subjugate the obdurate ego. This is called the first " mystical death " of the lower self, but it does *not* mean that the physical body then dies ! As every birth is preceded by a corresponding " death " on an adjacent plane, this cessation of the consciousness and dominion of the personality leads to a new birth on a higher plane of being. With this transfer of one's directive power and awareness to the higher self, or individuality, which Jesus described as being born again, there ensues an expansion of vision and understanding. The initiated one then begins to give back to the world that which he had previously acquired for the benefit of his own person.

This more generous attitude leads to the awakening of his heart quality and corresponds to Jesushood, manifesting as selfless service in various branches of worldly activity.   Then comes the second great initiation, of spiritual Baptism with the " descent of the Holy Ghost ;" this awakens the soul which was hitherto dormant.   Later there follows the Transfiguration known as the third degree, when the initiate realizes that he is an immortal being and his destiny is to become a true " son of God " with " life more abundant."

All these stages of inner unfoldment must find self-expression in the zest of normal earthly life, until the individuality is completely built up ; but during this period he remains a self-conscious being, separate from the Father. Slowly but surely he yearns and aspires more and more intensely for spiritual communion and realization of the Divine Presence.   However, the paradox is that the very attribute of individuality, which he has so strenuously developed and which is so gloriously unique and highly prized by each one, generates the veil that separates him from God. Really he is living in delusion, because God is Omnipresent and therefore is within and around him ; but he does not yet realize this truth. Gradually there arises within him an insistent urge for self-abnegation, and this increases until the initiate feels that nothing else matters, because he is famished by the lack of spiritual sustenance. To his appealing cry God responds with a compassionate welcome, though this is accompanied by the imperious demand that he must give himself fully and freely, without reservation, so as not to delay his return to the Father's Abode.

Every phase and feature of this period of mental grief and spiritual hunger is summarized in the agony of Gethsemane. Eventually the aspirant realizes the necessity of renouncing everything with unquestioned faith and confidence, knowing that he is immortal and that nothing can destroy his real being. But this means undergoing the second mystical death, that is, the renunciation of his higher self and the very soul of his cherished individuality.   Hence the cry of anguish : " Father if it be possible, let this cup pass from me."   At last, however, he recognizes there is no other way of release possible, so he consents, " nevertheless, not as I will, but as Thou wilt."

It is for our own future happiness and peace that this inexorable demand is imposed in order that we may become divine, for it was with purposeful intent that Jesus said : " Ye are Gods."   The full and final comprehension of this truth establishes a spirit of serene resignation within the initiate, that nothing in the world can disturb, although he must still face the inevitable course of events with imperturbable fortitude.   So he is tried and tested to the breaking point of his endurance, first by the cynical scenes of the Judgement Hall, then by the dreadful foreboding of the *Via Dolorosa*, and finally with the tragedy of Golgotha.   Truly appalling is this last act, for it is not sufficient that only one of his lower bodies be crucified, because his threefold personality, together with their counterparts of the higher self, are all subject to this voluntary self-sacrifice.   Actually he must make himself holy, that is whole, complete and spiritually exalted.   But the individuality, while still retaining its human nature, cannot fully understand what will yet transpire, and when :

> " the darkness covers the whole earth, and he gives up
> the Ghost,"

he feels that the light of his very soul is being extinguished, therefore he cannot repress the agonizing lament : " My God, my God, why hast Thou forsaken me ?"

Although the withdrawal of the inner light is " as death " to him, *he does not really die*, for this is merely the presage of a new and more glorious " birth."   The last remaining barrier between him and the Father is withdrawn when the " veil of the Temple is rent in twain " in order that he may realize the divine Light of his own spirit ; then he exclaims with ecstasy : " My Lord, how Thou hast glorified me !"

As this inner truth becomes fully manifest he proclaims : " I am he that was dead (to the Presence of God) but now I live for evermore " in Him. Thus the limited and segregated human soul becomes a conscious part of the Being of God, a Light of the Living Light that lighteth the entire Cosmos. Although the drop falls into the Ocean of Life, it does not cease to be a drop, yet it actually becomes one with the Ocean.

The Gospel records of the events that followed the Crucifixion vary considerably, but there is evidence of much that did transpire. Joseph of Arimathea was a nebulous character, brought into this drama in order to perform the service of veiling subsequent mysteries. Arimathea is undoubtedly a cypher name ; the word itself means : " a lofty character having an exalted state of consciousness," added to which the meaning of Joseph is : " God will give aid to increase me progressively, from perfection to perfection." The logical inference is that this name was employed as a pseudonym by the Master in order to cover his true identity after his suffering on Golgotha, because he was thereafter obliged to suspend his public Ministry and to live *incognito*. It is significant that Luke describes Joseph of Armiathea as : " a counsellor, and he was a just and good man," which are appropriate epithets for Jesus himself. The fact that he had the privilege of conferring with Pilate and secured permission to take the body from the Cross indicates that the Master had complete control over himself as a human being and so withdrew from public life.

Now it becomes more clear what is the true meaning of the :

"new sepulchre which was in the garden where he was crucified,"

for this is the " tomb which was empty," the person of Jesus void of every vestige of self. The stone which was placed at

the door of the sepulchre was the impenetrable silence that
the Master thereafter adopted to all, except his most intimate
disciples, but only the " Angel of the Lord," a synonym for
the soul, could roll away this stone of silence. Note
Matthew's description :

> " his countenance was like lightning and his raiment
> white as snow ;"

this is the state of the soul which was revealed at the Transfiguration, as being filled with spiritual light.

Having the faculty of prescience the Master was able to
instruct his disciples how best to care for his body and restitute
his health.   During his six hours of agony on the cross he
either fell into a coma or else withdrew his consciousness from
his physical form and entered into a trance condition, which
might well have been mistaken for death.   The record that
" forthwith came there out blood and water " as a result of
the piercing of his side by the soldier, demonstrates that his
circulation was not arrested, nor had the heart-beat ceased.
This episode is reminiscent of the " hierophant who touches
the heart with the thyrsus," the magic wand that was used in
the Ancient Mysteries and which liberated the soul of the
initiate from his human person.   Then he was able to descend
into the underworld and witness the condition of earth-bound
souls undergoing their necessary purgation in Hades.   He
could also ascend into heavenly heights and so meet angelic
hosts, saints and masters, and finally enter into the presence
of the Celestial Christ in his true being of Living Light and
Love.   Thereafter he was able to say : " All power is given
unto me in heaven and earth."

The sequence of events now becomes more illuminating :

> " Why seek ye the living among the dead ?   He is
> not here, he is risen ;"

meaning that his nature was no longer " dead," but it had

become spiritualized prior to reuniting with The Father, the word " dead " signifying the lower self.

> " Tell his disciples and Peter he goeth before you
> into Galilee, there shall ye see him."

The inference is certainly not geographical, but metaphysical, for as Galilee is the most northern region of Palestine, it is an appropriate metaphor to designate man's highest faculty, the soul. The actual meaning of this word is : " the plane and energy of the soul," and its specific use here is to show that in this realm of consciousness the Master can commune with his disciples. This idea is confirmed by the text : " in Galilee, into a mountain where Jesus has appointed them," which implies deep contemplation on the soul plane, corresponding to Samadhi. Otherwise it is inconceivable that he could only appear to his disciples in a secret place about one hundred miles north of Golgotha, for this would entail a very tiring journey lasting about a week, possibly on foot, and involve them in the difficulties of finding food and lodgings, when they were previously sent out " without purse or scrip " to preach the Gospel.

> " Yet a little while and the world seeth me no more ;
> but ye see me : because I live, ye shall live also. At
> that day ye shall know that I am in my Father, and
> ye in me, and I in you." . . .
> " He that loveth me shall be loved of my Father, and
> I will love him, and *will manifest myself to him.*" . . .
> " I said unto you, I go away, and come again unto
> you !"

Mary Magdalene was the first to visit the empty tomb " on the third day early in the morning." She personifies the redeemed love nature, and so was zealous in her desire to render homage and service to her Master. Note the stages of her progressive perception as his presence and inspiration are revealed, until she reaches the third plane of her higher self, the soul, designated as the " third day." " She cometh unto the sepulchre," the person of Jesus who is empty of self, " seeth the stone rolled away," because his veil of silence is drawn aside for her sake. " And as she wept she stooped down," lowered the state of her consciousness, " and saw two angels in white," representing the intuition and heart planes of Jesus, who bear witness that :

> " he is risen. They say unto her, woman why weepest thou ? and she said unto them, because they have taken away my Lord, and I know not where they have laid him. And when she had thus said she *turned herself back*, and saw Jesus standing, but knew not it was Jesus."

This shows that she had brought her consciousness down to the emotional plane by her grief.

> " Jesus said unto her, woman why weepest thou ? Whom seekest thou ? She, supposing him to be the gardener " (confirming the low plane of her consciousness) " saith unto him, Sir, if thou have borne him hence, tell me where thou hast laid him, and I will take him away."

Now follows a most significant and profoundly impressive verse :

> " Jesus saith unto her, *Mary* ; she *turned herself*, and said unto him, *Rabboni* ; which is to say Master !"

The exchange of these two words of greeting was overwhelming, and added to her " turning around " were sufficient to elevate her consciousness to the soul plane, where she felt the presence and heard the voice of the Master. In that state of devoted contemplation she desires to remain, but he explains that as he is still raising the level of his own consciousness she must not hold him back :

> " Touch me not, for I am not yet ascended to my
> Father, but go to my brethren and say unto them,
> I ascend unto my Father and to your Father."
> "Mary Magdalene came and told the disciples that
> she had seen the Lord, and that he had spoken
> these things unto her. Then the same day at
> evening, when the doors were shut where the disciples
> were assembled,"

indicates that they were all together in prayer and meditation;
and the " doors were shut " means that the lower senses were
closed against external distractions.

> " Jesus came and stood in the midst and said unto
> them, Peace be unto you."

Now follow the two most important verses in the Gospels :

> " Then said Jesus unto them, as my Father hath sent
> me, even so I send you. And he breathed on them
> and saith, receive ye the Holy Ghost ; whose soever
> sins ye remit they are remitted unto them !"

Observe first, there is the definite affirmation that Jesus and
the Father are two different beings, and that he was sent to
earth as His Representative. Only an initiate of the Master
rank, one who had attained God-realization and could therefore receive divine counsel and guidance, could fill this high
Office as the bearer of the Message of Truth. The second
major principle which is disclosed is that, by virtue of his
being such an advanced initiate, he was vested with power to
breathe a spiritual benediction upon his apostles, and so
transmit to them his delegated authority to bless, heal and
forgive ; this was real Ordination. Herein lies the secret
and mystery of the Apostolic Succession which, if rightly
understood, and exercised with the same spirit of selfless
devotion as the Master manifested, confers the power and
privilege to purify and uplift all who seek The Lord.

" Ye have not chosen me, but I have chosen you and
ordained you, that ye should go and bring forth
fruit."

An example of allegorical teaching is given by John when :

" Peter said unto the other disciples, I go a fishing.
They say unto him, we also go with thee.   They
went forth and entered into a ship immediately ;
but that night they caught nothing."

To " fish by night " suggests that they were trying to be
" fishers of men," although they were not yet fully qualified.
" But, when the morning was come," indicating a further
stage in their development, " Jesus saith unto them, children
have ye no meat ?"   To address them as " children " implies
their inexperience, and " meat " refers to spiritual sustenance
that was necessary to enable them to teach others.

" They answered, No ; and he said unto them, cast
the net on the right side of the ship, and ye shall
find."

A ship or boat represents the physical body, and the " right
side " means a positive and constructive attitude in presenting
the Teaching of the Master.

" And they were not able to draw the net for the
multitude of fishes ; and they drew the net to land
full of great fishes, one hundred and fifty three, and
yet the net was not broken."

This is a figurative description of the method the followers
of Jesus should adopt in giving the " good news," and shows
that part of the requisite training is to seek gems of invisible
Truth in the ocean of divine wisdom, which the fishes
symbolize.   The number 153 is an obvious cypher for 9,
and represents the fourth great initiation, as it also corresponds
to the " ninth hour " which precedes the attainment of

Masterhood—the fifth great initiation—and Union with the Heavenly Father, Whose symbolic number is 10.

> " Then said Jesus, come and dine, and he taketh bread and giveth them, and fish likewise."

This means he gave them further secret Teaching.

Another form of tuition adopted by the Master is revealed in his injunction to Peter :

> " So when they had dined " (or partaken of spiritual food) " Jesus said unto Peter, lovest thou me more than these ?   Peter replied, yea Lord, thou knowest that I love thee.   Then answered Jesus, Feed my lambs,"

meaning he was to give the simple ethical teaching to the first degree novitiates.

> " And Jesus said a second time, lovest thou me ? And Peter answered, yea Lord, thou knowest that I love thee.   Then he said unto him, Feed my sheep ;"

other translators write " yearlings," implying that there is a second grade of teaching, such as the inner meaning of the Parables, which is appropriate for accepted pupils. This standard is indicated by one who said : " I would see Jesus !"

> " And he said unto him a third time, lovest thou me ? And Peter was grieved because Jesus said unto him a third time, Lovest thou me ?"   (Had he forgotten his triple denial of the Master ?)   " Jesus said unto him, Feed my sheep !"

This last query suggests that the Christ Doctrines should be revealed to initiated disciples, such as those who ask : " where dwellest thou, O Christ ?"   Paul describes these three degrees by saying :

> " I have milk for babes, strong meat for men, but the Mysteries are reserved for the perfect ones."

The Apostles, being high initiates, were then empowered by Jesus to confer these three degrees of initiation, and give the corresponding tuition.

The Master then describes the difference between the normal man of the world and the one who has set his feet on the Path of Return :

> " When thou wast young thou girdest thyself, and walkedst whither thou wouldest : but when thou shalt be old, thou shalt stretch forth thy hands, and another shall gird thee, and carry thee whither thou wouldest not."

Thus he indicated that a young soul seeks to do what he likes and considers he has a perfect right to satisfy every mood and caprice of his person.   But when the soul becomes spiritually mature he must accept counsel from an elder brother on the Path, who may impose self-discipline and training that is not congenial to his person, though necessary for the liberation of his soul.

The Master then gives more explicit instructions to Peter : " and he said unto him, Follow me,"   The next verse of the text seems somewhat obscure :

> " Then Peter, *turning about*, and seeth the disciple whom Jesus loved, following."

To " turn about " suggests to direct the consciousness to higher planes.

> " Peter seeing him saith to Jesus, Lord, and what shall this man do ?"

Peter personifies the enlightened mind with faith, whereas John represents the heart quality and selfless love ; Peter is active and self-expressive, but John is a silent devotee.   Then Jesus answered :

> " If I will that he tarry till I come, what is that to
> thee ?   Follow thou me."
> " Whither I go thou canst not follow me now ; but
> thou shalt follow me afterwards."

How incisive are the words he addresses to the mind that is
conscious of its knowledge and logic, in contrast with his
appreciation of self-effacement and a loving heart.   One may
wonder whether the characters of these disciples are thus
depicted in order to represent different types, rather than
particular individuals.   To " tarry till I come " implies that
the state of Christhood may be attained during his lifetime,
though the Master's statement was then evidently misunderstood and materialized.   Therefore John seeks to
remove the incorrect assumption :

> " Yet Jesus said not unto him, *he shall not die,* but
> if I will that he tarry till I come."

This assertion : " he shall not die," seems to confirm that
physical death is not involved in the course of spiritual
progress.

> " This is the disciple that testifieth these things, and
> we know that his testimony is true."

John is the most mystical of the Gospel writers.   Some of
his most profound statements are not disguised as allegories,
but are definite expressions of spiritual truth.   Although his
language is simple, his substance is so abstruse that its deeper
meaning is often passed over unperceived.   Much that should
be understood as disclosing universal principles applying to
all mankind has been merely interpreted and propounded as
having a purely personal significance and application.

It has been wrongly assumed that the phrase :
> " I am the way, the truth and the life, and no man
> cometh unto the Father but by me,"

means that the spiritual destiny of all mankind, B.C. and A.D., was wholly and exclusively placed in the care of Jesus. The fuller meaning is that the inner experiences and initiations of the Master represent the most direct *Way* to the Heavenly Father ; the Christ Doctrines that he taught are an expression of the spiritual *Truth* of human advancement ; and his *Life* of selfless service to mankind with his utter devotion to God is the quickest means of achieving At-one-ment with The Father. However, such union is only man's immediate goal, but not the end of his existence !

Again : " In my Father's house are many mansions," indicates that there are many superphysical planes and states of being, suitable to all sorts and conditions of men, and wherein life ever continues. But can anyone ever reach and stay in a static condition that is for ever changeless ? Is not the Creator constantly active, constructing, transforming, improving and urging forward every living thing in the entire cosmos ? Is it possible, or even conceivable that when Jesus attained " At-one-ment with the Father " it meant such an exalted state of glory, power, wisdom and love that would make him equal to the Divine Perfection of Omnipotence, Omniscience and All-compassionate Love that embraces, governs and guides the numberless universes of Infinity and Eternity ? Surely he did not intend the words : " My Father " to refer to the Absolute Deity Who is the Great Architect of All ; otherwise he would not have qualified his words by saying : " The Father is greater than I."

The Absolute Godhead and The Father are not synonymous. As in this world there are many graduated stages and degrees of evolutionary progress, culture and virtue, so there are ever greater heights of consciousness in spiritual realms. Beyond the Master Jesus stands the Planetary Lord Christ ; beyond that wise and compassionate being is the Solar Heavenly Father of Love ; above him is the Cosmic Logos of the Universe, and finally there is The One in Whom all live and have their being. But undoubtedly there are many intermediary grades of spiritual beings, who are all ministers of God helping in the unfoldment and fulfilment of His Drama of Creation.

The mystery of the Ascension is therefore a graduated process of growth and advancement. One may progress and realize the Presence of God, but the sense of duality and separation remains. Even if one becomes God-conscious and perceives His attributes, he will still be an individual. Though one may be merged into the manifest Being of God the Creator and ever do His Will, one does not thereby become God. Only when one becomes entirely *non est*, and every faculty and feature of individuality is absolutely sublimated and transmuted into His Changeless and Unconditioned Bliss of Divine Light, Life and Love, the perfect Trinity in Unity, then only will one cease to exist in order To Be One with Him !

Regarding this enthralling quest Jesus encouraged us :

" I go to prepare a place for you ; I will come again
and receive you unto myself, that where I am there
ye may be also."

The unmistakable truth is that because he accomplished human perfection he is qualified to train, guide and initiate us to follow in his steps and experiences, so that we may reach the exalted state of Christhood, and pass on to still higher grades of consciousness. His assurance that :

" I will not leave you comfortless, I will come to
you,"

is also perfectly true. But alas, he has come again and again, though " his own received him not." Therefore he affirmed : " Other sheep (disciples) I have, not of this fold." Man only enters the Path of Return and Ascension, and begins his spiritual Journey to God, when he recognizes there are still unlimited degrees of Wisdom, Power and Glory awaiting his attainment. Every step forward is a source of increasing joy, peace and understanding :

" Lord, how is it that thou wilt manifest Thyself
unto us, and not unto the world ?"

" Jesus answered and said unto him : If a man love
me, he will keep my words ; and my Father will
love him, and we will come unto him and make our
abode with him."

" Your heart shall rejoice, and your joy no man
taketh from you !"

Apart from Paul and the Apostles, many saints and mystics
have since experienced this benediction, which has often been
accompanied by spiritual illumination.

" And now, O Father, I have manifested Thy Name
unto the men which Thou gavest me out of the world:
Thine they were, and Thou gavest them me ; and
they have kept Thy word, now they have known that
all things whatsoever that Thou gavest me are of
Thee."

The accredited Ascension of Jesus is inferred from the
simple words of Mark : " He was received into heaven ;"
but this does not even suggest that his physical body was
elevated into space. Luke merely says :

" While he blessed them he was parted from them,
and carried up into Heaven."

These statements may be compared with those referring to
Enoch : " who walked with God, and he was not ; for God
took him," and of Elijah it is written : " he was carried into
heaven by a whirlwind."

The spiritual aspect of the *Ascension* is that there must be a
reversal of the *Fall*, that is, of " the descent of Spirit into
matter," which was necessary in order that the divine Plan
of Evolution could be fulfilled. The obvious corollary must
be the eventual return of matter into Spirit, in order to
complete the Drama of Creation. As matter is crystallized
spirit, so spirit is etherealized matter. It is man's duty and

privilege to participate in this great work of transubstantiation, by his voluntary and conscious co-operation with God. Only by such intimate collaboration can a man become a Son of God and eventually at At-one with the Father. This mystical Ascension means the return of the human soul to the Creator, for thus it becomes divine : " though man in the form of man, he is God in the consciousness of God."

It was during this post-crucifixion period, when the Master lived in seclusion, that he gave to his most intimate disciples the profound tuition that transformed them into God-intoxicated men, and made them fearless martyrs for the sake of the Christ Message. The " Revelation of St. John " is a record of such secret training and initiation, and it is regarded as the key and seal of the Gospels. Jesus then also compiled the essential features of his principal parables, as well as the records of his own spiritual experiences which are known as the Great Initiations. These narratives constituted the mysterious " Quelle " manuscript which was the basis of the original Gospels. This teaching was known to members of the early Christian Society as the " Mysteries of Jesus," though it was not then lawful to reveal them.

The spiritual Drama of the Soul draws to a close with the assurance of Jesus :

> " These are the words that I spake unto you while I was yet with you, that all things must be fulfilled which are written in the law of Moses and by the Prophets, and in the Psalms concerning me."

This implies that the attainment of Christhood was foreseen, sought and partially accomplished by the most illumined of the Hebrew prophets.

The Church Father Clement wrote about 200 A.D.: " The Lord allowed us to speak of these Divine Mysteries and of that Holy Light, to those who were able to receive them, to the few to whom He knew they belonged." Moreover it is written :

" There is nothing secret which shall not be revealed, nor hidden that shall not be disclosed."

Jesus concludes :

" I have finished the work that Thou gavest me to do. Now O Father, glorify Thou me with Thine own Self, with the glory I had before the world was. Now I am no more in the world, . . . as I am not of the world."

Thus he acknowledges the Father is the Solar Being with Whom he was originally a part, and now, having completed his separate earthly pilgrimage, he is about to reunite with Him.

John, 16-28 :

" I came forth from the Father, and am come into the world ; again I leave the world, and go to the Father."

" All sorrow is vanished, death is vanquished, the deep Ocean of Joy fills thy spirit, and thy being is filled with Light, rare and untellable ; Light of the Very Light of God."

Such is the triumph of the Son's Ascension to the Heavenly Father.

It is Eternal Bliss to be At-one with Him.